# EYEWITNESS ● ART

# COLOUR

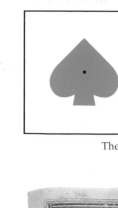

The "after-image" illusion

Moroccan rose and green tunic

The William Morris Window

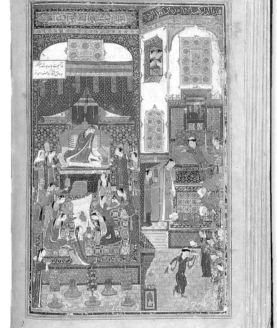

Persian manuscript illumination

Egyptian blue-glazed
ceramic of a god

Michelangelo, *Libyan Sibyl*, c.1508;
after restoration

Anish Kapoor, *As if to Celebrate I Discovered a
Mountain Blooming with Red Flowers*, 1981

# EYEWITNESS ◉ ART

# COLOUR

## ALISON COLE

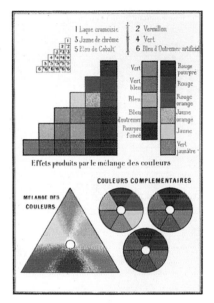

Frontispiece to Ogden Rood's
"Colours and Applications"

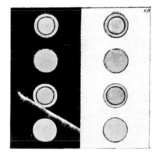

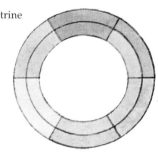

Details from
Goethe's "Doctrine
of Colours"

Sassetta, *The Wish of the Young St. Francis
to Become a Soldier*, 1437/44

St. Francis'
ultramarine
robe

Plastic palette with acrylic paints

**DORLING KINDERSLEY**
LONDON • NEW YORK • STUTTGART

IN ASSOCIATION WITH
**THE NATIONAL GALLERY OF ART,
WASHINGTON, DC**

Japanese Noh costume

Azurite

Lapis lazuli

Vermilion

Goethe's colour triangle

## A DORLING KINDERSLEY BOOK

**Editor** Luisa Caruso
**Designer** Claire Pegrum
**Assistant editor** Louise Candlish
**Design assistant** Simon Murrell
**Senior editor** Gwen Edmonds
**Managing editor** Sean Moore
**Managing art editor** Toni Kay
**Picture researchers** Julia Harris-Voss,
Jo Evans
**DTP designer** Zirrinia Austin
**Production controller** Meryl Silbert

**For the National Gallery of Art, Washington, DC**
Technical Consultants: Barbara H. Berrie, Conservation
Scientist; E. Melanie Gifford, Research Conservator for
Painting Technology

This Eyewitness ®/™ Art book
first published in Great Britain in 1993 by
Dorling Kindersley Limited,
9 Henrietta Street, London WC2E 8PS

A CIP catalogue record for this book is
available from the British Library

ISBN 0 7513 103 79

Colour reproduction by GRB Editrice s.r.l.
Printed in Italy by A. Mondadori Editore, Verona

Persian illuminated manuscript

Persian tiles with bird
and flower designs

Raphael,
*The Alba
Madonna,*
c.1510

Egyptian coarse
paintbrushes

Paul Signac,
*Portrait of
Félix Fénéon
in 1890,* 1890

# Contents

The three pairs of complementary colours

# What is colour?

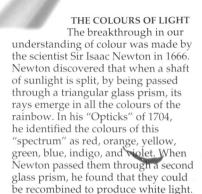

THERE ARE NO "REAL" COLOURS IN NATURE – only the various wavelengths that make up light, which are absorbed and reflected by all of the objects around us. The reflected wavelengths enter the eye, which, in turn, sends signals to the brain: only then do we "see" the miracle of colour. The sensation of white is created by the simultaneous impact of all these wavelengths on the eye. This white light contains the colours of the rainbow, which can be seen when the rays are separated by a glass prism. Each colour has its own wavelength: violet has the shortest and red the longest. When these colours are combined with nature's pigments – the chlorophyll in grass, for instance – millions of shades can be created. Painters reproduce these using the powdered colours of natural or artificial pigments (p. 62) – which are themselves only the colour of the light they reflect.

**THE COLOURS OF LIGHT**
The breakthrough in our understanding of colour was made by the scientist Sir Isaac Newton in 1666. Newton discovered that when a shaft of sunlight is split, by being passed through a triangular glass prism, its rays emerge in all the colours of the rainbow. In his "Opticks" of 1704, he identified the colours of this "spectrum" as red, orange, yellow, green, blue, indigo, and violet. When Newton passed them through a second glass prism, he found that they could be recombined to produce white light.

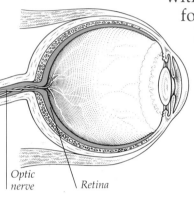

*Optic nerve*      *Retina*

**THE WORKINGS OF THE EYE**
Light enters the eye and hits the retina, where it is absorbed by rod and cone cells (so-called because of their shapes). These cells transmit the signals that light triggers via the optic nerve, directly to the visual centre at the back of the brain: colour is truly "in the mind of the beholder". The three types of cones are sensitive to red, blue, and green wavelengths, and seem to be responsible for colour vision in daylight. In dim light, the rods take over, which are more sensitive to blue-green light, and distinguish clearly between values of light and shade.

Painted colours, however bright, are always duller than the colours of light

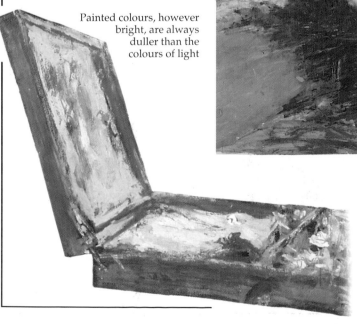

**STUDY FOR A PORTRAIT OF BONNARD**
*Edouard Vuillard; c.1930; 114 x 143 cm*
*(45 x 56¼ in); distemper on paper, mounted on canvas*
This study by the Post-Impressionist artist Edouard Vuillard (1868–1940) suggests the enchantment that colour holds for the painter. Vuillard has painted a fellow artist, Pierre Bonnard (pp. 48–49), standing in his studio, inspecting a brightly coloured landscape that he has just completed. The open paintbox (detail, left) represents not only the surface on which Bonnard has laid out his paints, but also his "palette" – the range of colours used. These consist of pigment (powdered colour) suspended in a liquid known as a "medium" (p. 62), which gives the colours their paint-like consistency.

## POLITICAL DRAMA
*Robert Delaunay; 1914; 88.7 x 67.3 cm*
*(35 x 26½ in); oil and collage on cardboard*

The 20th-century French painter Robert Delaunay (1885–1941) was intrigued by the way light could be broken up into the colours of the spectrum, and by the dynamic nature of light waves. These behave just like the electromagnetic wavelengths used by radio, which was a thrilling new invention in his time.

Here, the rainbow is pulled apart, and reassembled into a brilliant pattern of revolving arcs and rings. These mimic the impact of waves of light as they strike the eye, generating the same vibrating energy. Colours radiate outwards, like the ripples created by a pebble as it hits the surface of water.

ROBERT DELAUNAY

"Additive" mixture of primary lights

"Subtractive" mixture of primary pigments

### PRIMARY LIGHTS AND PRIMARY PIGMENTS

A century after Newton's "Opticks", it was discovered that white could be produced by mixing just three parts of the spectrum: red (orange-red), green, and blue (blue-violet) (above left). These primary lights can be "added" together to produce all possible colour sensations (red and green make yellow), and are also those to which the eye is most sensitive. However, when the three purest primary colours in pigment – used in modern colour printing and known as cyan (greenish-blue), yellow, and magenta (bluish-red) – are mixed, they produce black (above right). This is because pigment strongly "subtracts" or absorbs light, so that it only reflects the colour of the remaining wavelengths.

### HORSE
*Alexander Calder; 1970; height:*
*97.5 cm (38½ in), cut, bent, and*
*painted sheet metal; both sides*

For centuries, the colours red, blue, and yellow have been identified as the "primaries" of the painter. They cannot be created by mixing colours, and artists like Alexander Calder (1898–1976) delighted in their bright simplicity. These differ subtly from the purer printers' primaries described above, which are produced by mixing two primaries of light (above left).

### COLOUR DIMENSIONS

This colour star, by the 20th-century German painter and teacher Johannes Itten, is a version of Runge's sphere (p. 36), and classifies colour according to its three visual dimensions: "hue", "tone", and "saturation". "Hue" is what is known as colour: the star has 12 hues – the three primaries; the three secondaries (produced by mixing two primaries together); and the tertiaries (produced by mixing two secondaries). "Tone" is lightness or darkness, and "saturation" is "colourfulness" or intensity. Both of these can be altered by mixing colours with white or black.

# Ancient materials

THE COLOURS OF PREHISTORIC, Egyptian, and Roman painting reflect the rituals and symbols of their diverse cultures, as well as the limited range of materials that were available. The earliest pigments were made from naturally occurring coloured earths – white chalk, the reds, browns, and yellows from ochres, and darker umbers – and black charred wood. Dyes from animals and plants were soon exploited (although these colours often faded in light), as were the lasting, brilliant colours of minerals. To prepare paint, particles of pigment were ground into a "medium" – a binding agent like wax, egg, or tree resin – which made them workable and bound them to the paint surface. Synthetic colours, created via chemical processes, had also been developed by early Egyptian times.

### PREHISTORIC COLOURS
The cave paintings at Lascaux in south-west France, dating from c.12000 B.C. (above), reveal the earliest colours used by mankind. The main pigments, red ochre and black, symbolic of life (blood) and death, were usually created from red earth coloured by iron oxides, and burnt charcoal or bone. They were mixed with animal fats, then warmed to make them workable. Yellow ochre was also used, while the sparkling white of the calcite crystals that lined the walls of the cave was skilfully incorporated into the overall scheme.

### FOOD FOR A BANQUET
This Egyptian painting of the 19th Dynasty (c.1320–1200 B.C.), from the Tomb of Sennedjem, uses the typical Egyptian colours of white, black, turquoise, red, ultramarine blue (shipped from Afghanistan), and yellow ochre. The colours still appear so fresh and vibrant because they are mostly made from natural mineral substances, which do not have a tendency to alter or fade. The dead, for whom the tomb painters laid on this rich banquet, were later to feature in the creation of a colour of their own: "mummy brown", used for a time in the 17th and 18th centuries, was made from ground-up embalmed bodies!

Cinnabar mineral

Red ochre powder

Whelks, from which Tyrian purple was made

Block of yellow ochre, and ground powder

Charcoal

Malachite mineral

### ANCIENT PIGMENTS
These are some of the principal colours used by ancient civilizations. Stone Age man painted with charcoal, red ochre, and yellow ochre (the block above is freshly dug from the earth). The Egyptians ground the mineral malachite to make green (their colour for the Nile), while the Romans used a new bright red – discovered by the ancient Chinese – made from cinnabar. They also prided themselves on "Tyrian purple", a dye extracted from shellfish at Tyre in the Mediterranean, which came to symbolize wealth and imperial power.

Basalt palette and paint grinder, with "frits"

### EGYPTIAN EQUIPMENT
This palette and grinder were found in Thebes, along with coarse paintbrushes (right). They are shown with coloured "frits" (mixtures of chemicals used in glass manufacture), which were ground and mixed with gum, probably from the acacia tree. Another synthetic pigment was Egyptian blue (top right), a compound of silica, copper, and calcium. It is likely that this was borrowed from the glassy blue glazes that coated ceramics (far right).

# Flagellation Scene

*The Hall of the Mysteries, Pompeii; c.60 B.C.; fresco*

The dramatic red that enlivens the wall-panels of "The Hall of the Mysteries" is vermilion, made from cinnabar, which was used for the most sumptuous decorations. It was mined in Spain and was so expensive to buy that a law was passed setting a ceiling price. Apart from its prohibitive cost, cinnabar also posed technical problems, turning black on exposure to light. It had to be covered with a protective coat of wax and oil, which was then heated and polished with linen cloths and waxed cords.

### ROMANO-EGYPTIAN FUNERARY PORTRAIT

*2nd century A.D.; encaustic wax on panel*

This striking portrait was painted for the exterior of a coffin. Originally the head of the deceased would have been immortalized in stone, but painting was cheaper and could be remarkably life-like. Here, the sculptural character has been preserved through the "encaustic wax technique", in which burnt-in wax colours are handled with a fine knife to give a sense of depth and texture. The secret of this method was lost, although some have tried to re-invent it: it seems that beeswax was melted with an alkali, mixed with resin, and then colours were ground into it using a warm stone.

Egyptian blue

Blue-glazed ceramic of a god

Palm-fibre and twig brushes, c.1450 B.C.

Beeswax

# The splendour of gold

**ALTAR VESSELS**
Jewel-encrusted altar vessels –
like this French chalice of
the Abbot Suger of St. Denis
(c.1140) – were designed
to impress with their lustre
and opulence. The precious
gems and gleaming metals
multiplied the reflected light.

GOLD, THE MOST PRECIOUS METAL OF ALL, has been used by artists and craftsmen around the world to symbolize the glory of the heavens. Its colour – whether warmed by an underlayer of red clay or tinged with green from its natural impurities – gave an other-worldly quality to the sacred image, which seemed to rest on a bed of solid gold. In the Byzantine and medieval eras, the splendour of gold mosaic or gleaming burnished leaf represented two different levels of reality: the mystical realm of the heavenly sphere, and a pictorial world, created through suggestions of light and shade. When gold was illuminated by candles the effect was dazzling, inspiring religious wonder and awe.

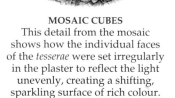

**MOSAIC CUBES**
This detail from the mosaic
shows how the individual faces
of the *tesserae* were set irregularly
in the plaster to reflect the light
unevenly, creating a shifting,
sparkling surface of rich colour.

**THE COURT OF JUSTINIAN**
The art of mosaic
flourished under the
rule of Constantinople
(Byzantium), in the so-
called Byzantine era (476
A.D. onwards). As distinct
from Greek and Roman
mosaics, which consisted
of *tesserae* (Latin: "cubes")
of marble set in plaster,
Byzantine mosaics were
created from coloured
glass. This allowed for
a richer range of colour,
including the use of
gold. In this mosaic
(c.574 A.D.) from San
Vitale in Ravenna, Italy,
gold unites the Empress
Theodora and the court
with the glory of god.

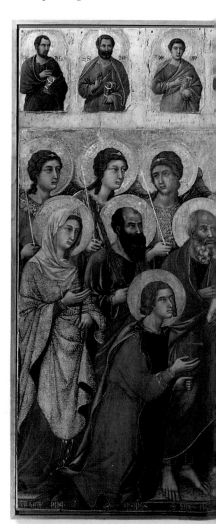

**THE ASCENSION OF MOHAMMED**
In this Persian manuscript (1539–43), gold is used to
invoke the spiritual splendour of the Prophet Mohammed's
ascension to Paradise. The flaming haloes behind the Angel
Gabriel and Mohammed burn brightly in the blue nocturnal
darkness. The Prophet's face is left blank – he is too holy to
be shown – and his dress is sober and unadorned. The red,
green, yellow, and blue of the angels' garments combine
to create an ecstatic play of colour across the page.

## Maestà (front)
### DUCCIO DI BUONINSEGNA
*1308–11; 214 x 412 cm (84¼ x 162¼ in); tempera on panel*
This, the front panel of the "super-altarpiece"
the *Maestà* (Italian: "Majesty"), was once the
glory of Siena Cathedral, Italy. Now dismantled,
it includes over 700 figures, but Duccio (active
1278–1319) and his workshop used only nine
pigments – three reds (one a red glaze), two
blues, green, black, white, and ochre – and
gold. The gold was lavishly applied, not only
to the background and haloes, but also to the
Virgin's throne and the Saints' richly brocaded
robes, to create webs of glistening highlights.

### ELABORATE BROCADE
This detail from the *Maestà* shows how precisely Duccio rendered the fabric of St. Catherine's cloak: fine white lines and gold twirls are painted over a greenish-grey base, and red is touched into the crosses. Each white line is meticulously edged with red, to make it stand out from the green.

### TEXTILE PATTERNS
This 14th-century Sicilian silk textile, inspired by oriental examples, reflects the Italian taste for intricacy of pattern and texture. Gorgeous fabrics, whether worn by the high clergy or the court, were considered to be a reflection of heavenly glory and the riches of God's creation.

*Parchment to protect the gold leaf from moisture*

*Diluted bole with brushes*

*Gesso ground*

### THE GILDER'S ART
Duccio's method of gilding a wooden panel is still used today. First, a number of thin layers of diluted bole (a reddish-brown clay) are brushed on to the prepared painting surface, known as the "ground", of white gesso (p. 62). The bole creates a cushion for the delicate beaten gold leaf, which is then applied in overlapping layers. Finally, the leaf is smoothed and polished with a burnisher – its tip made of a hard stone, such as agate (in Duccio's day, emeralds or rubies) – to give it brilliance and shine.

*Bole*

*Burnisher, with a hard agate tip*

*Smoothed gold leaf*

*Gold leaf – applied in overlapping layers*

# Fresco technique

THE ANCIENT ART OF TRUE FRESCO (Italian: "*buon fresco*") was revived by the great Florentine masters, Giotto (c.1267–1337) and Masaccio (1401–28). In this method of wall painting, powdered pigments are mixed with water and laid on a ground of damp plaster, which is made up of lime, with sand or marble dust. As the lime dries and the water evaporates, a hard crystalline surface is formed in which the colour is bound. This means that the colours have to be applied rapidly; otherwise, the hues can darken (Michelangelo even grumbled about his colours becoming "mouldy"). Many colours need to be avoided altogether, because they react chemically with the lime or water: vermilion and lead white, for instance, oxidize and turn black. Others, like azurite blue, must be applied "*a secco*" – that is, on dry plaster. As the fresco dries, all of the hues lighten – and this also has to be taken into account.

**THE TOREADOR FRESCO**
The Minoans – whose civilization ran parallel with that of the ancient Egyptians (c.2300–1100 B.C.) – seem to have been the first to use the true fresco technique. This mural from the Palace of Knossos in Crete, painted in about 1500 B.C., reveals a harmonious natural palette of pale yellow ochres and red iron oxides. These are mingled with other mineral pigments that evoke the colours of the Mediterranean sea.

**LAMENTATION OVER THE DEAD CHRIST**
*Giotto; c.1306; 200 x 185 cm (78¾ x 72¾ in); fresco*
Giotto's innovative fresco technique relied on the "dish system". Colours were mixed in separate dishes to his precise specifications: pure powdered colour, blended with water, would be prepared for the shadows, the same colour with white for the mid-tones, and the colour mixed with still more white for the lights. The accuracy of the dish system was very important, for the fresco was worked in daily sections of fresh, damp plaster, and colours had to be matched from one batch to the next. The hairline joins (detail, right) show these "*giornate*" sections (from the Italian: "*giorno*", meaning "day"). Apart from the sky, they tend to outline separate colour areas, which is why the figures are mostly clothed in robes of one hue.

**THE ARENA CHAPEL**
Giotto's famous fresco cycle of "The Lives of the Virgin and Christ" in the Arena Chapel in Padua, Italy, makes extensive use of the mineral pigment azurite. This beautiful blue colours the skies and runs like a thread through the entire narrative. It echoes the symbolic blue of the chapel vault, which represents the heavens. Unfortunately, azurite has to be applied *a secco*, which has made the blue particularly vulnerable: some patches have fallen away, while others have greened due to the reaction of the pigment with high levels of carbon dioxide.

## FRESCO LAYERS

True fresco is built up in layers on a dry wall. A mortar of coarse sand, lime, and water is applied on top, followed by a coarse plaster of three parts sand, and one part lime. Then comes the *"arriccio"*, another rough plaster, on which the fresco design (the *"sinopia"*, executed in sinoper, a red earth) is drawn. The smooth final layer, the *"intonaco"*, is only 3–5 mm (⅛ in) thick and is made up of sand or marble dust, and fine lime in equal quantities.

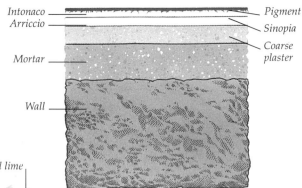

Intonaco — Pigment
Arriccio — Sinopia
— Coarse plaster
Mortar
Wall

Chalk
Bianco di San Giovanni
Slaked lime

Sinoper (red earth)  Raw umber

Raw sienna  Green earth

## CREATING FRESCO WHITES

Because lead white turns black in fresco, slaked lime (burnt lime combined with water) provides the finest fresco white, although chalk is also recommended in early manuals. Giotto used the paste known as *"Bianco di San Giovanni"*, a dried, ground lime treated with vinegar.

## FRESCO COLOURS

Since pigments derived from plants were sensitive to the alkali in the lime, fresco colours were fairly limited; earth colours were its staples (above).

## THE TRIBUTE MONEY

*Masaccio; c.1425; 225 x 598 cm (88½ x 235½ in); fresco*

Masaccio's recently restored fresco shows a palette of rich earth colours – roses, browns, oranges, and greens – combined with blue mixtures, lime white, and carbon black. He has chosen ordinary colours in the interests of naturalism and harmony; the coloured robes flow into each other (their hems seem to elide), or are subtly contrasted: blue, for instance, against green. There are no outlines to interrupt the suggestion of light and space, and no brilliant colours (p. 62) applied *a secco*.

## TIEPOLO'S DECORATIVE COLOURING

The radiant frescoes painted in the 18th century by the Venetian painter Giambattista Tiepolo (1696–1770) still feature a surprisingly small range of colours. In his frescoes for the Würzburg Palace in Germany (left), painted in 1751, a wealth of sunny colours complements the superb architecture of white, gold, and patterned marble. Many of these are inspired mixtures: the warm oranges are Tiepolo's own blends of simple red and yellow pigments.

## ST. JOHN

Masaccio has given his apostles tanned complexions so that the "white" light falling on the skin is more sharply defined. In this detail, the undermodelling (p. 62) in green shows through the flesh, especially in the areas of shadow.

# The value of colour

IN EARLY ITALIAN PAINTING, colour symbolism was an eminently practical affair. While some theorists tried to associate the different colours with the planets or the four elements of nature – red for fire, blue for air, green for water, and grey for earth – the artist was led by more pragmatic concerns. The most important factors, for the artist and the patron who commissioned him, were the quality and cost of the colours. Ultramarine blue, the jewel of them all, was extracted from the lapis lazuli stone, after it had been quarried and shipped from Afghanistan – its name *"oltremarine"* means "from across the seas". Because of its costliness, ultramarine was used for the most significant figures in the artist's narrative, the finest grades being reserved for Christ and the Virgin. The only colours that equalled ultramarine in intensity were vermilion, used for other key players, and pure gold.

**PREPARING ULTRAMARINE**
After being crushed in a mortar, lapis lazuli was incorporated into a mixture of viscous materials, such as oils and honey, wrapped in a cloth, and kneaded with an alkali – all to extract its violet-blue.

Lapis lazuli

Vermilion

Azurite

**THE BRIGHTEST RED**
An artificial vermilion was developed from sulphur and mercury, and became one of the most reliable pigments. It was bought by the lump, and then ground, to make sure that it had not been secretly mixed with red lead or brick.

**THE CORONATION OF THE VIRGIN**
*Enguerrand Quarton; c.1453–54; 183 x 220 cm (72 x 86½ in); tempera on panel*
Many contracts drawn up between the patron and painter specified the use of only the best-quality pigments. The detailed contract for this altarpiece states that the main blues must be ultramarine, although cheaper "German" blue, azurite (above), could be used for the frame. The finest ultramarine adorns the robe of the Virgin, which is echoed in the deep blue sky below. The use of blue, gold, and vermilion relates to the different levels of Christian devotion: gold and red were associated with the worship of the Trinity, Saints, and angels; and blue with the Virgin.

Bronze Florentine scales

14th- and 15th-century florins

**WEIGHING IMPORTANCE**
Colours were sold by the weight. The finest grades of ultramarine, distinguishable by their deep violet undertone, were sold at two to four florins an ounce. Blue at four florins to the ounce might be stipulated for the Virgin, while one florin to the ounce would do for the rest.

# Colour symbolism

During the early Renaissance period (14th and 15th centuries), colours were considered to exist in a symbolic hierarchy. Their importance was dictated both by value and by the "divine" status accorded to pure, brilliant hues. This was a continuation of the medieval idea that bright, clear colours are a reflection of the beauty of God's creation, while mixed colours are "corrupted". Aside from this, colour was used according to the fashionable tastes and the story-telling conventions of the time. Saints, for instance, were often identified by the colours of their robes, while other meanings could be understood from the way that colour was used in context.

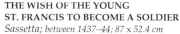
**THE WISH OF THE YOUNG ST. FRANCIS TO BECOME A SOLDIER**
*Sassetta; between 1437–44; 87 x 52.4 cm (34¼ x 20¾ in); tempera on panel*
St. Francis' charity is emphasized by the fineness of the robe he is giving away – in pure ultramarine. This colour is echoed in the star-spangled canopy above his bed of gold, where he dreams of the religious order he is to found (this episode of the story appears in the same panel). The combination of blue and gold was often identified with Christianity.

Ultramarine

Yellow ochre

**THE CRUCIFIXION**
*Masaccio; 1426; 83 x 63 cm (30¼ x 25¼ in); tempera on panel*
The startling red robe belongs to the grieving figure of Mary Magdalene. She was the Holy Woman who witnessed Christ's crucifixion, and mopped his bleeding feet with her flowing hair. Her robe is the colour of his blood – the blood of sacrifice and martyrdom. From ancient times onwards, red has been associated with blood and life: Chinese "ox-blood" red vases were once used in sacrificial rites. Ultramarine also plays an important role in the narrative, drawing attention to St. John the Evangelist's grieving gesture (on the right).

Vermilion

**THE KISS OF JUDAS**
*Giotto; c.1305–6; 200 x 185 cm (78¾ x 72¾ in); fresco*
Giotto uses yellow ochre for the voluminous robe of Judas Iscariot, the disciple who betrayed Jesus to his enemies with a kiss. This colour not only attracts the eye to the focus of the composition, but is also associated with evil and, more specifically, betrayal and cowardice. The meaning of this colour would have been clear to Renaissance viewers. Other shades of yellow were used to identify St. Peter (Lorenzo's altarpiece, p. 16) and St. Joseph (Lippi's *Adoration*, p. 17). In non Christian cultures, yellow has different associations: it was worn by the Emperor in Imperial China, while to ancient Hebrews, the yellow of the chrysolite gem gave protection from envy.

# Egg tempera painting

THE COLOURS OF early panel paintings (from the 13th century to the late 15th century) are often beautifully preserved. This is because they are, in the main, painted in egg tempera – wet pigment (powdered colour in water) bound in a medium of whole egg (sometimes just egg yolk). As the proteins in the egg harden, the colours acquire a sheen as soft as velvet and a skin as tough as shell. However, the watery content of the egg limits the range of pigments and the way they can be used. Because the water evaporates quickly, the paints begin to set almost immediately. This means that the colours are not at all easy to blend, and have to be mixed beforehand in pure or simple combinations. Nor can the paint be applied thickly to create effects of texture, for it tends to shrink and crack. Colours must be painstakingly applied in thin, filmy layers, using light brushstrokes that will not lift the sticky paint lying underneath.

## CENNINO'S HANDBOOK
"The Craftsman's Handbook" (c.1400; above), written by the Florentine painter Cennino Cennini, provides a detailed account of egg tempera techniques. These were based on a system of modelling (p. 62) figures in light and shade: pure colour was used in the shadows, and lead white was added towards the highlights.

Ready-mixed egg tempera

Gesso (for grounds)

Egg yolk

Size (animal glue)

Whole egg

## THE EGG MEDIUM
Tempera painting demands that the artist has a good knowledge of the materials. Cennino even recommends using the paler yolks of town hens so that they do not affect the clarity of the colours (he added that the redder yolks of country hens might be useful for painting swarthy or aged flesh tones).

## REVERSE OF PAINTED PANEL
Tempera paintings are mostly executed on panel – a support made of white poplar (above) or other suitable woods. The panel was covered with several coats of glue made from animal-skin clippings (known as "size"), so that the wood would not absorb the paint. It was then prepared for painting with a brilliant white ground, made of gesso.

## THE CORONATION OF THE VIRGIN
*Lorenzo Monaco; c.1414; wings: 181.6 x 104.8 cm (71½ x 41¼ in); central panel: 217.2 x 115.6 cm (85½ x 45½ in); tempera on panel*
This radiant altarpiece illustrates one of the main advantages of the Cennino system of modelling in white – the unnatural brightness of the colours. The altarpiece would have shone in its original dark church setting, with vivid pinks, yellows, greens, and blues easily holding their own against the metallic gold. Following the usual procedure, Lorenzo first completed the gilded areas, then the draperies, furnishings, and, finally, the flesh. The Virgin's white robe was once a deep pinkish-mauve: Lorenzo used a red lake glaze (p. 22), which has faded away in the light.

This "*tondo*" (Italian: "round painting") marks a transition between the old and new styles of colouring

## THE ADORATION OF THE MAGI
*Fra Angelico and Filippo Lippi; c.1445; diameter: 137.2 cm (54 in); tempera on panel*
The brilliance of tempera colour, with its limited range of pure and premixed shades, made it perfect for representing the spiritual world, but not so suitable for rendering naturalistic settings. This picture was painted in the 15th century, when the new perspective system was transforming art, and the Renaissance theorist Alberti was urging artists to darken their colours with black towards the shadows, so that objects seem to recede. Here, the "old-fashioned" brightness of the figures contrasts markedly with the more subdued, realistic colours of the dulled landscape.

## PREPARING COLOURS
Pigments were freshly prepared by an assistant, and bound with egg at the last possible moment. This French manuscript illustration (1402) shows the pigments, which came in lump form, being ground in water on a hard stone slab. Some colours had to be ground coarsely to keep their intensity. Brilliant hues, like ultramarine, vermilion, and gold, were used alongside colours like lead-tin yellow, malachite (green), vine black, and lead white.

Vine black

Lead tin yellow

Malachite

Fresco flesh colours

Verdaccio

Cinabrese

Sinoper

Detail of St. Catherine, from Duccio's *Maestà* (pp. 10–11)

## FLESH PAINTING
The only complex layering of colour in tempera occurred in the areas of flesh. In this, tempera echoed fresco practice, in which an underpaint of "*verdaccio*" (a greenish mixture) was worked over with flesh colours: the pale red ochres – sinoper and cinabrese – mixed with lime white. In tempera, "*terra verde*" (Italian: "green earth") or *verdaccio* was used for the ground, followed by lead white tinted with vermilion.

## VIRGIN AND CHILD WITH ST. ANDREW AND ST. PETER
*Cima da Conegliano; c.1500; painted area: 47.8 x 38.9 cm (18¾ x 15¼ in); unfinished tempera and oil on panel*
This unfinished painting stands at the crossroads of the old tempera and new oil techniques (pp. 22–23). Italian artists of this period often still used tempera for the initial modelling (as in the figure on the left), because it is fast-drying. The underpainting was then glazed over with oil. Although oil soon replaced the old method, egg tempera is valued and used to this day.

### GREEN FACES
This cross-section of flesh clearly shows the underpaint of green earth. In tempera paintings like the *Maestà* (detail, above), the top layer has worn down, leaving a greenish cast.

# Colour, light, and narrative

JUST AS INDIVIDUAL COLOURS could be invested with symbolic meaning (pp. 14–15), so a particular "style" of colouring could be used to reflect the story or theme of a picture. This was largely a matter of decorum or appropriateness: that is, the style of colouring had to suit the nature of the subject painted. Leonardo da Vinci's dark, atmospheric manner (pp. 20–21) was particularly effective for dramatic or tragic subjects, while brilliant "*cangiante*" colouring (Italian: "changing") – in which unnaturally bright colours shift from one hue to another across their surface (p. 62) – was often used for supernatural revelations. Piero della Francesca (c.1410/20–92) chose a limited range of colours to give his complex narratives clarity. For naturalistic subjects, the "harmonious" style of subtly blended tones was considered to be a judicious choice.

## SUPERNATURAL COLOUR
The popular German painter Matthias Grünewald (c.1460–1528) was renowned for the dynamism of his colouring. In his *Resurrected Christ* (below right), Christ – traditionally dark-haired and bearded – is transformed into a golden-haired figure with glowing red eyes. In this detail, his face dissolves in a blaze of light – from which his features emerge in all their dazzling beauty.

### THE RESURRECTED CHRIST
*Matthias Grünewald; c.1510–15; right-hand panel of triptych: 269 x 143 cm (106 in x 56¼ in); oil on panel*
This panel from the Isenheim altarpiece in Germany, illustrating the joy of Christ's Resurrection, vividly contrasts with Grünewald's darkly expressive scene of crucifixion (far left). Christ's skin is white, free of all taints of sin and suffering, apart from the gleaming red stigmata (marks left by the nails of his crucifixion). He trails a radiant *cangiante* cloth: the white is "shot" through with blue, in the manner of shot silk (p. 62), which miraculously changes to blazing hues of rose, orange, and pure yellow. These colours are echoed in the halo of light around Christ's head. Below, the earthbound soldiers, painted in duller earth colours, stumble and flounder, blinded by the light.

### THE SMALL CRUCIFIXION
*Matthias Grünewald; c.1511/20; 61.3 x 46 cm (24¼ x 18¼ in); oil on panel*
Sombre colours – gangrenous greens, midnight blues, and deep reds – convey the anguish of the crucifixion. In the livid light, Christ's pale green, bloodless figure is exposed in all its agony. His mother's blackened garments express the intensity of her grief, while Mary Magdalene's robe forms a pool of blood red.

### BRIDGET'S VISIONS
Grünewald was greatly inspired by the mystical "Revelations" of St. Bridget of Sweden, a text of stark and visionary intensity. This engraving is after a miniature in a 14th-century edition.

### THE ANNUNCIATION
*Piero della Francesca; c.1455; 329 x 193 cm (129½ x 76 in); fresco*
This fresco is part of a cycle illustrating the "Legend of the True Cross" – the cross of Christ's crucifixion. Piero alludes to the cross structurally and symbolically, using a restrained palette of rose, dark green, white, brown, and blue that emphasizes the different levels of the narrative. The fresco is divided into a Latin cross, formed by the architecture: the upright of the white pillar and "arms" of rose and green marble. In the spaces between, the monumental figures of God and the Virgin echo each other in rose and blue, while the beam across the open window is mirrored by the brown cross-beams of the door below – both of which refer symbolically to the cross.

**THE ALBA MADONNA**
*Raphael; c.1510; diameter: 94.5 cm (37¼ in);*
*oil on panel, transferred to canvas*
Raphael (1483–1520), who was a master of different styles of colouring, chose a low-key harmony of tones (further muted by a layer of yellowed varnish) for this gentle theme. Red and ultramarine are subdued to blend the Madonna with the soft landscape colours, for this is the "Madonna of Humility", who is always shown seated on bare ground.

**THE ADORATION OF THE SHEPHERDS**
*El Greco; 1612–14; 319 x 180 cm (126 x 70¾ in); oil on canvas*
El Greco painted this ecstatic scene for his burial vault in the church of San Domingo el Antiguo in Toledo, Spain. He chose to set the scene in the dark cave setting mentioned in the early Book of James, but filled it with silvery supernatural light. As in St. Bridget's vision, this radiance emanates from the Christ child, illuminating the pale flesh tones and deep, saturated colours of the draperies of the figures. It also picks out the sun-baked features of the elderly shepherd kneeling in the foreground, who is thought to be a self-portrait of the artist.

**MYSTICAL UNION**
The colours of the draperies – red, orange, blue, gold, and green – form two glowing circles around the newborn Christ: the earthly sphere, represented by Mary, Joseph, and the shepherds; and the angelic sphere, in a halo of brightness above. By spiralling colours upwards in an inverted "S" shape, from the orange on the shoulder of the shepherd, the eye is drawn into the spiritual heart of the composition, where Heaven and Earth are joined.

# Leonardo's naturalism

THE ITALIAN RENAISSANCE MASTER Leonardo da Vinci (1452–1519) applied his remarkable intellect to the science of vision, colour, and light. By gaining universal insights from the tiniest details of nature, such as the coloured veins in pebbles or the light on wind-blown leaves, he created a new ideal of naturalistic colour. He developed *"chiaroscuro"* – a method of painting using light and shadow (pp. 30–31) – whereby forms suffused in light seem to emerge in three dimensions from darkness. The more subtle *"sfumato"* (Italian: "smoky") technique, in which colours and contours are softened by smoky shadows, was his own invention. In landscape backgrounds, Leonardo practised his "aerial" perspective (p. 24), imitating the way nature's hues become bluer over distance, as they penetrate atmospheric mists and vapours.

**Glass for "considering colour mixtures"**

**THE RAINBOW COLOURS OF NATURE**
Leonardo enthusiastically explored the colours of the rainbow in his notebooks (left). Its myriad hues were observed in bubbles of water, peacock feathers, "the roots of turnips kept in stagnant waters" – surrounded by rainbows of reflected light – and "antique glass found underground". As a practical guide to seeing the infinite colour mixtures in nature, he suggested looking at countryside through pieces of coloured glass, to see which of nature's colours would be "impaired" or "improved" by blending. Yellow and green glass were found to enhance colour the most.

**STUDIES OF LIGHT AND SHADE**
Leonardo stated that "the scientific and true principles of painting first establish what is a shaded body [form], and what is light". He made exhaustive studies of the effects of sunlight and shadow on the colours of trees and leaves (above), from which he formulated general rules. He took into account the thickness of the branching, the dappling effect of shadow, and even the shape of the leaf itself.

**GINEVRA DE' BENCI**
*Leonardo da Vinci; c.1474; 38.8 x 36.7 cm (15¼ x 14½ in); oil on panel*
In this early portrait, Leonardo uses *chiaroscuro* to create a sense of relief that rivals the roundness of sculpture – the figure seems to project from the picture surface. He also reveals the painterly contrasts between smooth, luminous flesh, soft, lustrous curls, and dark, spiky juniper leaves. Brilliant colours are banished, for Leonardo believed that a painting "may be adorned with ugly colours, and yet astonish those who contemplate it, through the appearance of relief".

**SOFTENED LANDSCAPE**
This landscape detail from *Ginevra* shows Leonardo exploring Flemish advances in oil technique (p. 22). The shifts in colour – created by translucent glazes – enhance the effect of distance, the palest blue being furthest away.

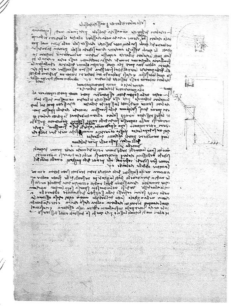

## VEILS OF TRANSPARENCY

Leonardo's painting shows his concern with transparency. Thin glazes cast a "veil" of atmosphere over the landscape; and painted veils adorn St. Anne's forehead and reveal the Virgin's bare arm. The dark area in the foreground may have once been a clear pool.

## ULTRAMARINE SICKNESS

The strange, milky flatness of the blue robe worn by the Virgin is possibly due to "ultramarine sickness". This is caused when the pigment comes into contact with an acid, from any source, and loses its colour entirely.

## COLOURED PEBBLES

Small coloured pebbles, like those at St. Anne's feet, were of special interest to Leonardo. From their patterned formations of coloured minerals, he learned about larger geological structures and the intricacy of natural colour harmonies.

## DOMINATING BROWN

A strong, brownish underpainting, often consisting of bitumen brown (below), gave a sculptural foundation of light and shade that Leonardo allowed to show through his colours. Most other dark brown tones are due to the browning of copper-based greens, like verdigris (below), a problem that the artist wrote of in his notebooks.

## The Virgin, Infant Jesus, and St. Anne

LEONARDO DA VINCI *after c.1507; 168 x 130 cm (66¼ x 51¼ in); oil on canvas*
This late painting is a lovely example of Leonardo's delicate *sfumato* technique. Shadows are blurred in a mist of smoky colour and outlines have disappeared. The expressions on the faces hover between soft light and shadow, while the figures in this gentle scene fuse together in natural harmony, and seem to move and breathe. Even the shifts of colour in the mysterious, rocky landscape are virtually imperceptible.

A bottle of bitumen brown

Verdigris

# Colouring in oils

THE REFINEMENT OF OIL PAINTING in the early 15th century opened up an almost unlimited range of colour possibilities. In this technique, the powdered pigment is mixed with a slow-drying oil – such as linseed or walnut – which absorbs oxygen from the air, forming a transparent skin that locks the colour in. This means that oil paint can be built up in many layers, and applied opaquely (thickly, so that light cannot penetrate it), semi-transparently, or in transparent glazes (usually thinned with glossy turpentine or resins). Because the oil dries slowly, the "edges" of colours can also be blended and fused easily. Early on, artists exploited the smooth transparency of glazes, which allow light from a luminous underlayer to shine through. Colours could be modified simply by varying the under-paint, transparency, or order of layers: in one painting only three or four pigments were used to create over 20 different shades of red and pink! Later, artists began to explore the rich textural possibilities of oil paint in an increasingly free and personal manner.

Walnut oil    Linseed oil

Walnuts

### THE OIL MEDIUM
The oils most frequently used by the Old Masters were linseed and walnut. These dry slowly – unlike olive oil, for instance, which never dries – and form a flexible surface. Linseed was particularly valued by Van Eyck (below right) for the smooth, jewel-like brilliance it gave to colours. Walnut oil is thinner (Leonardo suggested that it should be left in the sun to thicken), but it does not yellow as much as linseed – oils often turn yellow or brown with age.

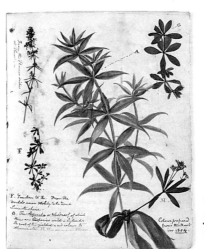

### LAKE PIGMENTS
Lake pigments – organic ink-like dyes deposited in a powder base, such as chalk (p. 62) – were often used as oil glazes, since, when mixed with a binding medium, they become translucent. Madder lake is a lovely transparent red made from the roots of the madder plant. Carmine, from crushed cochineal insects, makes an exquisite (if perishable) crimson glaze. Yellow lakes, derived from berries, fade in oil and are best avoided.

Carmine

Cochineal insects

Yellow lake

Madder roots from the madder plant (illustration, far left)

Buckthorn berries

### WET-IN-WET
These close-up details are from Van Eyck's *Annunciation* (far right), but after its 1992–93 cleaning. The threads in the Angel Gabriel's green brocade robe were skilfully stroked across the green under-layer while it was wet.

Gabriel's green robe (after cleaning)

### RICH GLAZING
This detail from the Angel Gabriel's red velvet mantle shows how Van Eyck uses red glaze over a full-bodied opaque underpaint to suggest the richness and texture of the fabric. Small cracks in the paint reveal the white ground beneath.

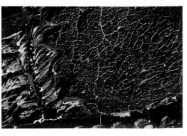

Gabriel's red mantle (after cleaning)

### THE ANNUNCIATION
*Jan van Eyck; c.1434–36; 90.2 x 34.1 cm (35½ x 14 in); oil on canvas, transferred from panel*
In his own lifetime, the Flemish painter Jan van Eyck (c.1390–1441) was celebrated as "the inventor of oil painting" – although drying oils had been used since at least the 8th century. However, Van Eyck did develop the technique to an astonishing degree, exploiting the optical properties of super-imposed layers of glazes to create an endless variety of subtle light effects. Working on a reflective white ground, he applied glassy transparent layers so that the light would penetrate and bounce back off the white to the eye. For the shadows, he used multiple layers of thicker glaze to deepen and enrich the colours, rather than muddying them with black.

## TARQUIN AND LUCRETIA
*Titian; 1568–76; 182 x 140 cm*
*(71¾ x 55 in); oil on canvas*
The great Venetian painter Titian
(c.1487–1576) vigorously exploited
the new freedom and flexibility of
the oil technique. He described this
late picture, showing the brutal rape
of Lucretia by the King of Rome,
Tarquin, as the product of much
"labour and artifice". Analysis of
the painting has shown that Titian
changed both the colouring and
composition as he worked (right),
and made other alterations over the
three years in which it was kept in
his studio. The colours are applied
in incredibly complex layers, often
including contrasting hues (p. 39).
In the reddish-green curtain, for
example, blue and green mingle in
the shadows. Titian was never afraid
to "dirty" his colours, as he put it,
to produce richer natural effects.

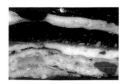

### THE COUNTERPANE
In this cross-section, the
change from orange-red
to green seems to be
due to changes in the
colour scheme made by
Titian as he painted.

### TARQUIN'S BREECHES
The deep red is built up
in layers: red lead, thick
pink and white *impasto*
(p. 62), and red glazes.

### X-RAY VISION
This X-ray enables
us to look beneath the
surface of the painting
(the lead in Titian's
pigments absorbs the
rays). It reveals the
changes made by Titian
in the composition –
most obviously the
shift in position of
Tarquin's dagger
and right arm.

Lead white
pigment
shows up
in X-rays

## MINERVA PROTECTS PAX FROM MARS ("PEACE AND WAR")
*Peter Paul Rubens; 1629–30; 203.5 x*
*298 cm (80 x 117¼ in); oil on canvas*
The works of the 17th-century
master Rubens (1577–1640) reveal
the full potential of oil painting.
The luminosity and soft fluidity of
colour were thought to be due to
the use of lustrous resins, although
they are now attributed to Rubens'
dazzling painting skills. He uses
fresh and simple colour mixtures,
painting his shadows thinly so
that he does not dull their
transparency and warmth.

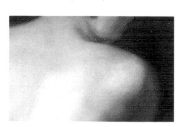

### COLOURED SHADOWS
In the flesh, warm glazes are
interspersed with strokes of pale
grey, blue, and green to suggest
the coloured lights in the shadows.

# Colour and space

Colour and light are powerful tools in the creation of a sense of space. Tones can be gradually shifted from dark to pale, creating subtle gradations of brightness that the eye follows into the distance. The nature of colour itself can be exploited – reds tend to advance and blues tend to recede. These effects have been explained by optical science (p. 33). But our perception of space and depth in landscape is also influenced by an external phenomenon: in nature, colours lose their intensity and distinctness at a distance because of the increasing body of air or "atmosphere" through which they are seen. The short wavelengths of blue light (p. 6) travel through this "veil" of air more easily than the longer wavelengths of red, which is why colour appears paler and bluer towards the horizon. The colouristic device that mimics these effects is known as "aerial" or atmospheric perspective.

**ARTFUL LIGHT**
In this idyllic Pompeian landscape, from the mid-1st century A.D., light enters from the side, illuminating the golden facades of shrines and temples, and dissolving distant forms in hazy violet-grey shadow. The impression of light and depth is enhanced by the use of green and brown – "local" colours (p. 62) – in the foreground, as opposed to the unreal, pastel hues of the background.

Detail of blue landscape

**THE REST ON THE FLIGHT INTO EGYPT**
*Gerard David; c.1510; 41.9 x 42.2 cm (16½ x 16¾ in); oil on panel*
This landscape by Gerard David (c.1460–1523) moves in gentle steps from the warm greys and ochres of the foreground rocks to a pale lemon-green clearing, where Joseph is busy knocking down chestnuts. The more abrupt transition to the cool blues of the distant landscape (created by lead white tinted with azurite; detail, left) is masked by dark bushes.

**LANDSCAPE WITH HAGAR AND THE ANGEL**
*Claude Lorrain; 1646; 52.7 x 43.8 cm (20¾ x 17¼ in); oil on canvas, mounted on panel*
Claude Lorrain (1600–82) developed a foolproof formula for creating the type of landscape that it seemed the viewer could "walk through". The effect was created by framing the landscape with a dark foreground and tall trees that acted like stage wings (left). These wings open on to a luminous middle distance, with a stretch of water leading the eye back into space. The subtle colour transitions follow the rules of aerial perspective, moving from a misty townscape to pale, far-away hills.

## THE DOGANA AND SANTA MARIA DELLA SALUTE

*J.M.W. Turner; c.1843; 62 x 93 cm (24½ x 36¾ in); oil on canvas*

J.M.W. Turner (1775–1851) was fascinated by diffused sunlight – particularly at dawn – as can be seen in this radiant Venetian view. In Venice, Turner could use his favoured palette of white, luminous yellows, pinks, blues, and greys to create a shimmering vision of light and space – without having to touch the "nasty" greens he abhorred. The golden mass of the landing jetty and the dark diagonal of the moored gondolas lead the eye into a floating space that is only defined in our imagination. Its glassy greyness is brought to life by hints of pure colour.

Prussian blue

Naples yellow

### CONSTABLE'S GREENS

When Constable began painting, the green pigments available were dull and disappointing (the bright emerald green only appeared in 1814), so he created his green colour mixtures from Prussian blue and Naples yellow (far left).

Detail of green landscape

### WIVENHOE PARK, ESSEX

*John Constable; 1816; 56.1 x 101.2 cm (22 x 40 in); oil on canvas*

In contrast to Turner, John Constable (1776–1837) used a great variety of greens to create this exceptionally spacious landscape. Constable was anxious to suggest space through natural colours like grass-green, rather than employing the artificial range of hues used in aerial perspective, which usually ranged from mellow reddish-browns to silvery pale blues. Nevertheless, his khaki foreground, warmed by small accents of red, is still close to the brown traditionally used by artists such as Claude (far left), while blues are visible in the sunlit greens of the background.

# The Venetian School

THE VENETIAN PAINTERS of the 16th century were renowned for their dazzling way with colour. While their fellow countrymen in Tuscany continued to paint in bright colours isolated by firm outlines, the Venetians chose to confine themselves to a range of exceptionally rich and pure pigments, applied in blended patches. The quality of their colours was largely due to Venice's position as a leading maritime port. Built on a shimmering lagoon, she traded in luxury goods, importing cargoes of exotic spices, rich silks, jewellery, scents, and new dyes and pigments from the Eastern Mediterranean. While artists from all over Italy sent to Venice for foreign pigments, the Venetians received them first and made their novelty into a speciality. But it was the way that they handled these colours that set the Venetian painters apart. As well as delighting in the brilliance of the pigments themselves, they subtly balanced, mixed, and interwove them in the interests of "truth" and harmony, using colour saturation and brightness to suggest natural light effects. As a consequence, the figures and settings merge in a haze of light and atmosphere.

**THE PALACE OF GOLD**
Venice's passion for colour and precious materials was reflected in her architecture. The Byzantine *"Pala d'Oro"* (Italian: "Palace of Gold") was encrusted with gold, enamel, and jewels: this section from the *Pala d'Oro* (1105) shows Christ in Judgement. Other palaces were adorned with coloured marbles or frescoes. "He that will row through the Grand Canal," wrote a visiting Englishman, "shall see [houses] more like the dwellings of princes than private men."

**BIRD'S-EYE VIEW OF VENICE**
Venice's position as "queen of the sea", with a large Mediterranean empire (stretching from Istria, to Crete and Cyprus), made her the richest and most powerful city in Italy in the 16th century. The quality of her imported goods was unrivalled: the ultramarine used by the leading Venetian painter of the time, Titian (below), is of the highest purity and intensity.

**DANAE**
*Titian; 1553; 127.5 x 178 cm (50¼ x 70 in); oil on canvas*
This late work by Titian – depicting the rape of Danaë by the god Jupiter (in the form of a shower of gold) – shows the vigorous originality of his handling of the brush. Strokes of different colours are placed side by side, which only blend together when they are viewed at a distance. Varieties of paint texture interact with the weave of the canvas to emphasize the contrasts between the energetic shower (detail, below), the golden-skinned Danaë, and the mottled body of the old maid.

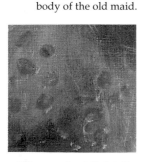

"Shower of gold" detail

# The Family of Darius before Alexander

**PAOLO VERONESE** *c.1570s; 236.2 x 474.9 cm (93 x 187 in); oil on canvas*

Paolo Veronese (c.1528–88) was the master of the Venetian "narrative" – large canvases that decorated walls in much the same way as fresco. Since they were painted in oil, there were no colour limitations, but Venetian artists chose to limit their palette to a small number of hues. Veronese delighted in creating unusual, blended colour mixtures ("broken" colours) from this range. His famous "Veronese green" (above) is created from a solid green underpaint (verdigris, lead-tin yellow, and a little malachite) with a copper resinate glaze.

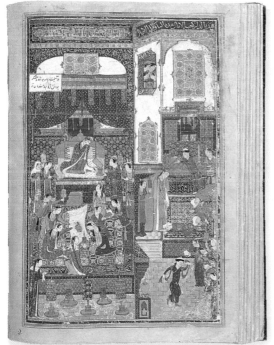

### COSMETIC COLOUR
Painters often heightened the reds of flesh tones (detail, right) with vermilion, or glazes made from red lakes such as madder or brazilwood (far right). This partly reflects the liberal use of rouge by Venetian women; rouge was made from brazilwood or dragon's blood (a tree resin). As an artistic practice, it was frowned upon by Vasari, the Renaissance art historian, who complained that it "falsifies the freshness of living flesh".

Detail from Titian's *Tarquin and Lucretia* (p. 23)

Dragon's blood

Brazilwood

Madder

### EASTERN PIGMENTS
The Venetians borrowed two beautiful pigments from manuscript painters of the East: realgar (orange-red) and orpiment (yellow). These regularly appear in Persian manuscript illuminations, such as this one, and surface in Venetian painting in the 1490s. Realgar provided the Italians with the first true orange (previously they had mixed red and yellow), and the two pigments combined produced glorious reddish-golds.

Realgar

Orpiment

### POISONOUS PIGMENTS
Realgar (arsenic sulphide) and orpiment (yellow arsenic trisulphide) are two of the most poisonous pigments.

Verona green

Charcoal black

Venetian red

### LOCAL RESOURCES
Painters also valued relatively dull local colours, such as green earth (from Verona), charcoal black, and Venetian red.

### THE DYER'S TRADE
Venice was a major centre of wool and silk dyeing. New colours were continually being developed, along with more permanent fixatives. People clothed themselves in a variety of shades, which often echoed the broken colours of Venetian painting: "*flammeo*" (Italian: "flame"), for example, hovered between orange and gold.

# The restoration of colour

THE RECENT CLEANING of the frescoes by Michelangelo (1475–1564) in the Sistine Chapel in Rome has caused widespread controversy over the true colours of Old Master paintings. Original colours are often obscured by the grime of centuries, and are sometimes even completely distorted by "repaints", where restorers of the past have tried to match the colours to the tastes of their own times. In the 19th century, collectors liked their pictures to have the warm, dark tones of a Rembrandt (p. 31): *The Feast of the Gods*, by the Venetian masters Giovanni Bellini (c.1430/40–1516) and Titian, was overpainted where it had been damaged, and given a layer of varnish – its yellowing later subdued the colours further. Now, restorers try to re-create the original appearance of a painting, using the latest technology to analyse the pigments and binding media.

**MICHELANGELO'S EVE**
This unrestored detail of Eve from the Sistine Ceiling shows that animal glue was brushed over the fresco, darkening the colours. A triangular area has been missed, revealing the original, brighter hues.

**THE LIBYAN SIBYL**
*Michelangelo; c.1508; fresco; detail of the Sistine Ceiling*
When Michelangelo's restored Sistine Ceiling was revealed, it caused a critical uproar. Before cleaning, the dusky colours (left) were described as "sculptural" rather than painterly, echoing the brooding, "melancholy" temperament of the artist. After cleaning, these ideas had to be abandoned. As the restored *Libyan Sibyl* (far left) shows, Michelangelo was not only a wonderful colourist, but also a pioneer in this field. Never before had *cangiante* colouring (p. 18) been used on this scale. The dynamic, shot hues (p. 62) of the draperies give the figures a spiritual energy and beauty, in keeping with the optimistic spirit of Renaissance Christianity.

Michelangelo's *Libyan Sibyl*, after the restoration of the Sistine Ceiling

**THE FEAST OF THE GODS**
*Giovanni Bellini and Titian; 1514/1529;*
*170.2 x 188 cm (67 x 74 in); oil on canvas; before restoration*
In 1568, Vasari described this painting as "one of the most beautiful works that Giovanni Bellini ever created". Vasari added: "... unable to carry through this work because he, Bellini, was old, Titian was summoned, since he was better than all others, so that he might bring it to completion." X-rays of the painting from the 1950s confirm that Titian had substantially repainted the landscape. The discoloured resin varnish was only removed in 1985, revealing glorious Venetian colour.

## The Feast of the Gods

**BELLINI AND TITIAN** *as left; after restoration*
When the layer of varnish was stripped away, it was found that, in the early 19th century, all of the draperies of the figures had been toned down. Some of the foliage had also been thickly overpainted, to give it the golden glow so admired at the time. Few were prepared for the brilliance and variety of the colours that emerged. The brooding landscape was transformed into a sunlit glade, filled with air and movement, while the gods appeared in an array of rich draperies. Rose pinks, blues, oranges, and other bright shades appear alongside shot hues, like those of the splendid crimson and pale turquoise tunic, worn by the helmeted god, Mercury.

**BLUE AND WHITE PORCELAIN**
The restoration has revealed the delicate detail and lustre of the Chinese porcelain (similar to this 16th-century Medici ware), held by the satyr and nymph.

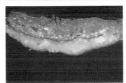

**SILENUS' DRAPERY**
These cross-sections of paint samples were removed during cleaning. Here, thin orange-red ochre paint lies over the original realgar and orpiment of Silenus' robe (figure on left).

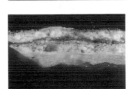

**CYBELE'S DRESS**
Cybele's salmon pink dress (centre) is composed of lead white, vermilion, and red lake. There are crimson glazes in the shadowy folds, with touches of yellow in the lights.

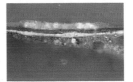

**PRIAPUS' DRAPERY**
This sample from Priapus' shot drapery (second figure from right), shows varnish on an opaque red-orange layer (vermilion with iron oxides), over a transparent green.

# Chiaroscuro: light and shadow

**CANDLELIGHT**
Some artists painted by candlelight to achieve a *chiaroscuro* effect, while others worked by the "red" of a blazing fire.

*C*HIAROSCURO – LITERALLY "BRIGHT-DARK" (Italian) – was an effect pioneered by Leonardo (pp. 20–21), which focused on dramatic contrasts of light and shade. While Leonardo used it primarily to model forms, artists like the great Italian painter Caravaggio (c.1571–1610) exploited it in the interests of narrative and spiritual impact, thrusting his figures into the spotlight and allowing the deep shadows to mould and engulf their forms and features. Such daring colouristic effects can be compared to the manipulative lighting of vintage Hollywood movies. Caravaggio's influence was enormous. In the 17th century, Georges de La Tour (1593–1652) used the exaggerated *"tenebroso"* (Italian: "dark") technique of Caravaggio's later years to create images of stillness, while Rembrandt (1606–69) explored the painterly drama of light and shadow. Later, Edouard Manet (1832–83) was inspired by the pure contrast of light and dark tones.

**THE CALLING OF ST. MATTHEW**
*Caravaggio; c.1597–98; 322 x 340 cm (126¾ x 133¾ in); oil on canvas*
This startling scene was painted for the Contarelli Chapel in the church of San Luigi dei Francesi in Rome. The chapel is very dark, but Caravaggio avoided the brilliant hues favoured by his contemporaries, choosing a limited palette of blacks, blues, and whites, and using warm earth colours that would glow in the chapel's gloom. One fellow painter, Carracci, commented that Caravaggio "ground flesh" to make his earth pigments. Here, Matthew (the tax gatherer) and his friends are seated at a tavern table, their rich costumes contrasting with the poor garments of two barefoot figures on the right. The shrouded, enigmatic figure of Christ is identified by his strong gesture, illuminated by a dramatic shaft of light from the side.

**OUT OF DARKNESS**
The light on the figures of Christ and St. Peter (detail, right) gains its amazing spiritual power from the impenetrable black shadow that throws Christ's face and hand into sharp relief and bites into their forms. The flesh is shadowed – no match for the brilliantly illuminated face of Matthew's young companion – but, against the black, it glows with a simmering intensity.

**THE REPENTANT MAGDALENE**
*Georges de La Tour; c.1640; 113 x 92.7 cm (44½ x 36½ in); oil on canvas*
De La Tour often painted intimate nocturnal scenes, where strong contrasts were created by candlelight. In this newly restored painting, the candle is partly obscured by the dark form of the skull, but its flame illuminates the pensive figure, bringing out delicate tones of shell pink, white, copper, and brown. Her slender hand is silhouetted, and the light shines through the rosy flesh of her fingers (detail, right).

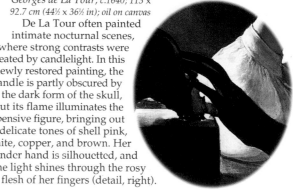

## A WOMAN BATHING IN A STREAM

*Rembrandt; 1654; 61.8 x 47 cm*
*(24¼ x 18½ in); oil on panel*

This sensual painting was probably made for Rembrandt's private enjoyment. The direct application of paint shows particularly clearly how Rembrandt achieved his rich light effects. The panel is primed (p. 62) with a warm yellow-brown – visible in the unpainted strip on the lower curve of the woman's shift – that glows through the pigments. It is combined with wonderfully thick strokes of white and grey in the shift, and the yellow and orange ochres of the robe, to suggest light and texture. The shadows are described by dark tones, as well as alternating "warm" and "cool" colours; reddish tones give an impression of warmth, while bluer tones seem cool (p. 62). Here, they are used to give the flesh a sense of roundness.

### A MODEL IN THE ARTIST'S STUDIO

The effect of studio lighting on colour was a major consideration. In this drawing by Rembrandt (c.1655), the studio window is fitted with a canopy so that the artist can control the light. Rembrandt's contemporary, Sandrart, observed that some studios were so filled with sunshine that the colours became "diminished and confused". He recommended north-facing windows with blinds or adjustable shutters to give a "richness of shadow and reflection".

Burnt umber    Burnt sienna    Spanish brown

### REMBRANDT'S PALETTE

Rembrandt's palette was rich in earth pigments – ochres, umbers, and siennas. These were cheap, stable, and could be used raw, or roasted (burnt) to give richer or warmer shades, before mixing with oil.

### CREATING BLACK

Manet's "lively" blacks have been found to include bright colours ivory black was even mixed with red lake, cobalt blue, and orange (left).

### STILL LIFE WITH MELON AND PEACHES

*Edouard Manet; c.1866; 69 x 92.2 cm (27¼ x 36¼ in); oil on canvas*

The great 19th-century master Manet chose a stark frontal lighting, as opposed to the lighting from the side that was favoured by so many of his predecessors (far left).

This head on approach flattens the forms, allowing Manet to omit the in-between tones of traditional *chiaroscuro* and paint in unmodulated areas of lights and darks. He explained his effects: "Don't bother about the background. Look for the values. When you look [at a still life], when you want to render it as you see it ... you don't see the stripes on the wallpaper."

# Painting with light

THE DUTCH PAINTER JAN VERMEER (1632–75) was fascinated by light and its painted effects: the lustre of shiny surfaces, the highlights on skin and textured fabrics, and the depth of colour in shadow. Like the French masters Jean-Baptiste Chardin (1699–1779) and Henri Fantin-Latour (1836–1904), Vermeer was intrigued by the effect of light on hue and tonal values (p. 7) – for example, the way blues lighten in dim daylight conditions, while reds appear particularly bright in intense light. All three painters sacrifice detail to light, describing the imperfect way we actually see. Chardin even blurs the face of his figure in *A Lady Taking Tea*, to make sure that the viewer's eye roves naturally over the picture.

**OPTICAL IMAGES**
Vermeer's preoccupation with light, colour, and texture led to his use of a room-type "camera obscura" (above). The camera – a darkened cubicle with a pinhole, through which light entered – produced a condensed image of the subject to be painted on a screen or wall. The image appeared in miniature: the effects of light and shade were dramatically contrasted, while colours took on a crystalline clarity and intensity.

## The Girl with the Red Hat

JAN VERMEER *c.1665; 23.2 x 18.1 cm (9¼ x 7 in); oil on panel*
In this small, jewel-like painting, the unfocused, "photographic" nature of the image points to the use of a camera obscura. Vermeer seems to have traced the projected image and then copied the broad pattern of lights and darks directly on to his panel. He then built up the colour tones using numerous thin layers of glazes, so that the pigments appear to be suspended in glass. For the hat, he used vermilion of a remarkable intensity, enhanced with red lake.

Lead white reflects the light

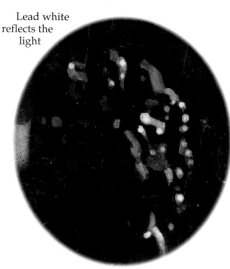

**GLOBULES OF LIGHT**
In the camera obscura image, small, gleaming highlights on foreground objects melt together and spread into unfocused globules of light. Vermeer has reproduced this effect using thick dots of lead white on the sculpted brass ornaments of the chair, which are in the shape of lions' heads (detail, above).

## A Lady Taking Tea

JEAN-BAPTISTE CHARDIN *1735; 80 x 101 cm (31½ x 39¾ in); oil on canvas*
Chardin creates different planes of soft light by subtly varying the degree of distinctness and brightness of the objects depicted. The points of highest illumination are the back of the woman's head – her face is veiled in shadow – and the hand in front of the cup. The foremost plane is defined by hue, in the brilliant red of the lacquer cabinet, which seems to advance towards us, just as the blues seem to recede. This is an optical effect: to focus on red (behind the retina), the lens of the eye becomes convex, and, as a result, the colour appears larger and nearer. In the case of blue (focused in front of the retina), the lens flattens, and the colour appears further away.

### STILL LIFE

*Henri Fantin-Latour; 1866; 62 x 74.8 cm (24½ x 29½ in); oil on canvas*
Fantin-Latour uses a single source of light to unite objects of a variety of colours and textures: the brittle porcelain, the coarse-skinned fruit, the satin-soft camellias, the basket, vase, and book are all subjected to its modifying effects. There are subtle variations of brightness or intensity, when an object is highlighted or shaded. These are calculated according to its colour under normal lighting conditions.

**FINE-TUNING COLOUR**
When a colour comes into shadow, Fantin-Latour alters it consistently and proportionately, in a delicate process of colour adjustment. The arrangement is disrupted only by the cast shadows (thrown by one object on to another) and the bright reflections (detail, right).

*Reflected light*

*Cast shadows*

# Rococo decoration

FRENCH ROCOCO STYLE developed in the early 18th century as a reaction to the high-mindedness of classically inspired art. It derives its name from the rock-and-shell work (French: "*rocaille*") that decorated garden grottoes. In 1699, the art historian Roger de Piles shocked the French art world by championing colour and spontaneity at the expense of "design" – the classical method of composition based on drawing, favoured by the establishment. In the debate that followed, de Piles won the day and French artists, like François Boucher (1703–70) and Jean-Honoré Fragonard (1732–1806), set about adapting the majestic colours of Titian and Rubens to the light, amorous atmosphere of society drawing-rooms and boudoirs.

**LOVE AS CONQUEROR**
*Jean-Honoré Fragonard; c.1775; oval: 55.9 x 46.7 cm (22 x 18¾ in); oil on canvas*
This decorative oval reflects the playful frivolity of French 18th-century taste. The rosy tints, which caress the flesh, flowers, and clouds, are the enchanted hues of dawn and love.

**HOLLYHOCKS**
*Jean-Honoré Fragonard; 1790–91; 318 x 63.5 cm (125¼ x 25 in); oil on canvas*
These Chinese-style canvases (left; far right) were painted to decorate the salon at the house of Fragonard's cousin. Their slender grace and airiness is achieved through a type of vertical aerial perspective (p. 24); the eye is swept upwards from warm pinks and umbers, through fresh whites and yellows, into clouds of misty foliage.

Chinese porcelain covered jar, with "Famille Rose" decoration

Sèvres pot-pourri vase, c.1759

**THE BOUCHER ROOM: THE ARTS AND SCIENCES**
This whimsical room decoration was commissioned by King Louis XV's mistress, Madame de Pompadour, for her library at the Château of Crêcy, and was completed in about 1750 to 1752. The designs for the panels were probably intended to be used for tapestry chair covers, and the "chocolate box" colours echo the artificial pastel blues, greens, and rosy pinks of Beauvais tapestry shades. Boucher had been producing designs for the Beauvais factory since 1734, and was later to become Inspector of the Gobelins tapestry works (far right).

**PORCELAIN BRILLIANCE**
The 18th-century craze for everything Chinese also influenced Boucher's colouring. He loved the pinks, sea greens, and turquoise-blues of Chinese porcelain (the jar, far left, dates from the Ch'ing Dynasty of 1644–1912). These were imitated in the Sèvres porcelain glazes of his day (left).

**A YOUNG GIRL READING**
*Jean-Honoré Fragonard; c.1776; 81.1 x 64.8 cm (32 x 25½ in); oil on canvas*
Aside from his decorative works, Fragonard was famous for the dash and spontaneity of his portraits. He could adapt his palette accordingly, using pale, silken tints for his decorative commissions, and vivid, Rubensian colours for pictures, like this one, in his "rapid manner". Here, the background is sketchily brushed with bitumen brown, so that the figure, in glorious daffodil yellow, seems to bloom before our eyes. The sunlight bounces off the soft lilac cushion, which is so thinly painted that the radiance of the off-white top layer of ground shows through. Its burnt umber shadows add to the overall impression of warmth.

**GOBELINS TAPESTRY**
Both Boucher and Fragonard produced designs for the highly successful Gobelins tapestry factory in Paris. This involvement carried through to their decorative paintings, where the graceful colours of Gobelins wall-hangings and furnishings were often deliberately echoed, so that the whole scheme of the room would harmonize. The influence was two-way: after Boucher's death, Gobelins workers weaved a succession of tapestries based on his paintings, such as this one, after his *Cupid and Psyche*.

*Lapis lazuli*

"A Tint Book of Historical Colours Suitable for Decorative Work": Gobelins tints

**ROCOCO FURNITURE**
Fine furniture, like this gilded tripod table with its lapis lazuli top (c.1785), also contributed to an atmosphere of luxury and elegance. The gold was echoed in gilded frames and stucco decoration, while the semi-precious lapis lazuli stone hit a note of pure, unashamed extravagance. Boucher himself collected rare furniture, fragments of lapis lazuli, rock crystals, gems, porcelains, enamel, and mother-of-pearl, revelling in their pretty, sparkling colours.

*Gilt bronze*

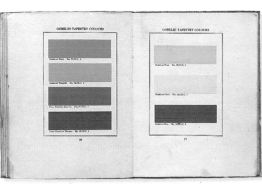

**DECORATIVE SHADES**
This book of historical tints, used by paint manufacturers to define colour combinations, shows some of the famous Gobelins colours. As Inspector, Boucher introduced a wonderful variety of fresh, delicate shades to match the Rococo spirit of design. His paintings were transformed by this interest: he flattened his colours and restricted their range, heightening the transparency of lights and virtually abandoning the rich colour of shadow.

# Goethe's colour theory

In 1810, THE GREAT GERMAN WRITER Johann Wolfgang Goethe (1749–1832) mounted a scathing attack on Newton's "Opticks" in his *"Zur Farbenlehre"*, "The Doctrine of Colours". Goethe opposed Newton's discovery that there were seven colours of the spectrum (p. 6) with his own theory that there were only six, which were seen under natural daylight conditions. To him, colour was composed of lightness or darkness: thus yellow was the first colour to appear when white was darkened, and blue was the first when black was lightened. Although these ideas were not borne out by physics, Goethe was himself a painter, and his interest in the way we actually see and experience colour greatly stimulated later theorists and artists. He observed, for instance, how yellow sunlight produces deep violet shadows, and he described the positive and negative effects of colour on the mind.

**GOETHE'S DIAGRAMS**
The first plate of *"Zur Farbenlehre"* includes Goethe's colour wheel (top left) and several diagrams devoted to distorted colour perception. The little landscape at the bottom shows how people who cannot perceive blue see the world around them.

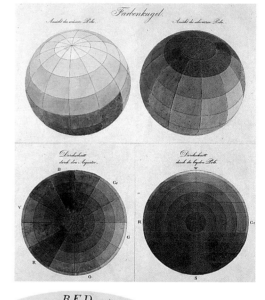

**RUNGE'S SPHERE**
The German painter Philipp Otto Runge (1777–1810) shared Goethe's interest in the way colour could be used in painting. His colour sphere (1809), shown here at different angles, establishes a way of measuring pigment colour. Colour wheels like Goethe's show relationships between hues, but Runge also grades his hues in a scale from light to dark, and saturation to "greyness" (p. 7).

**MORNING (EARLY VERSION)**
*Philipp Otto Runge; 1808; 109 x 85.5 cm (43 x 33¾ in); oil on canvas*
Like his contemporary Goethe, Runge explored the symbolic and spiritual relationships between colours. In *Morning*, these are revealed through the harmonious contrast of golden yellow light and shadowy purple-blue (p. 39). "Colour," he wrote, "is the final art, which is, and will always remain, a mystery. It contains the symbol of the Trinity. Light or white is the good, and darkness is the evil ...".

**PRIMITIVE COLOURS**
Before Goethe and Runge, the scientist and naturalist Moses Harris produced a colour wheel (c.1770) that emphasized the "primitive" or primary colours – red, yellow, and blue (right). The idea of three primary pigment colours had emerged in the 1720s, but it was not truly accepted by most artists until the mid-19th century.

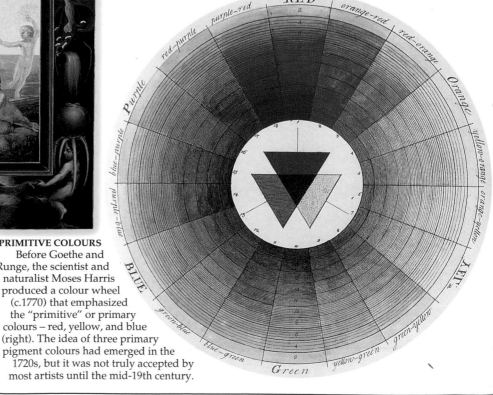

## COLOURS OF THE SPECTRUM

Goethe's watercolour shows the results of two experiments of light passing through a prism: the colours on the left include the three main colours of Newton's spectrum – orange, green, and violet – which would have been perceived in a dark room from a controlled ray of light; the ones on the right represent Goethe's principal spectral colours – blue, red (which he called *purpur*, meaning "peach blossom"), and yellow – seen by the eye in daylight. With the other colours in this strip – green, blue-red, and yellow-red – these six hues form the basis of Goethe's colour circle (below).

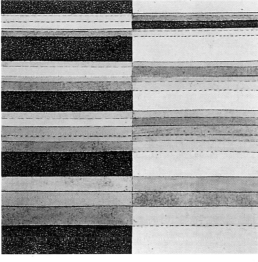

## EASTLAKE'S EDITION

In 1840, Goethe's theory was translated into English by the painter Charles Lock Eastlake (title page, right). The great landscape master Turner seized on it, marking his copy with typically bluff notes. What attracted Turner was Goethe's pairing of contrasting colours – which centred on the opposition of yellow and blue – into "positive and negative", "warm and cold", "brightness and darkness", and "light and shadow".

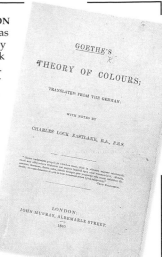

## GOETHE'S COLOUR CIRCLE

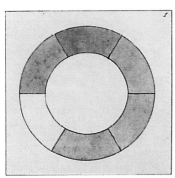

Goethe's wheel was formulated around pairs of colours: yellow and blue; yellow-red (orange) and blue-red (violet); and red and green. For the painter's purposes, red was considered to be as fundamental as his two primaries, yellow and blue. Contrasting colours appear opposite each other: Goethe had observed how green, for instance, produces an after-sensation of red (p. 45).

## LIGHT AND COLOUR (GOETHE'S THEORY) – THE MORNING AFTER THE DELUGE – MOSES WRITING THE BOOK OF GENESIS

*J.M.W. Turner; 1843; 78.7 x 78.7 cm (30 x 30 in); oil on canvas*

Turner composed a verse to accompany this picture: "... Th' returning sun Exhaled the earth's humid bubbles, and ... Reflected her lost forms, each in prismatic guise ...". Turner has transformed the entire composition into a "bubble", filled with glowing, prismatic hues. Goethe's lively "positive" colours – yellow, red-yellow (orange), and yellow-red – dominate. When Turner was asked what the painting meant, he replied simply, "Red, blue, and yellow."

## SHADE AND DARKNESS – THE EVENING OF THE DELUGE

*J.M.W. Turner; 1843; 78.7 x 78.1 cm (30¾ x 30 in); oil on canvas*

In 1843, Turner exhibited a pair of paintings (above; above right), which were influenced by Goethe's theories. The viewer was provided with a vivid and idiosyncratic illustration of Goethe's "positive" and "negative" forces of colour, and the conflict between light and shadow. Here, the dark sky and seething waters of the Biblical flood are swept into a whirling mass of blacks and purple-blues, surrounding a pool of yellow light in the distance. These colours – yellow and blue – are placed opposite each other in Goethe's colour wheel to show that they complement each other by contrast (pp. 38–39). According to Goethe, they symbolize the external forces of God and nature, over which humanity has no control.

## THE MATERIALS OF THE ARTIST

Turner was one of the first to distinguish between the artist's materials – painters' pigments (Turner's own box of colours is shown here) – and the material of the physicist – light. Turner realized that when the artist mixed his primary colours, the result was a muddy grey, while the prismatic primaries produced white light (p. 7).

# Harmony and contrast

THE LEADING FRENCH Romantic painter Eugène Delacroix (1798–1863) and the chemist Michel Eugène Chevreul (1786–1889) had an immense influence on artistic colour-practice. Individually, they developed a new idea of colour harmony based on contrasts, which was totally opposed to the traditional method of harmonizing and darkening colours with layers of warm-toned varnish. Noticing, like Leonardo and Goethe before them, how harmonies in nature, and in optical science, are achieved through bright contrasts – the green shadows in rosy flesh, for example – they wove together highlights and shadows in webs of complementary colours. Both men arrived at their ideas from differing standpoints: Delacroix from the bravura examples of Veronese and Rubens, combined with his experience of North African light, and an admiration for Constable's landscapes; Chevreul from his work supervising the strength and colour of dyes at the Gobelins tapestry workshop.

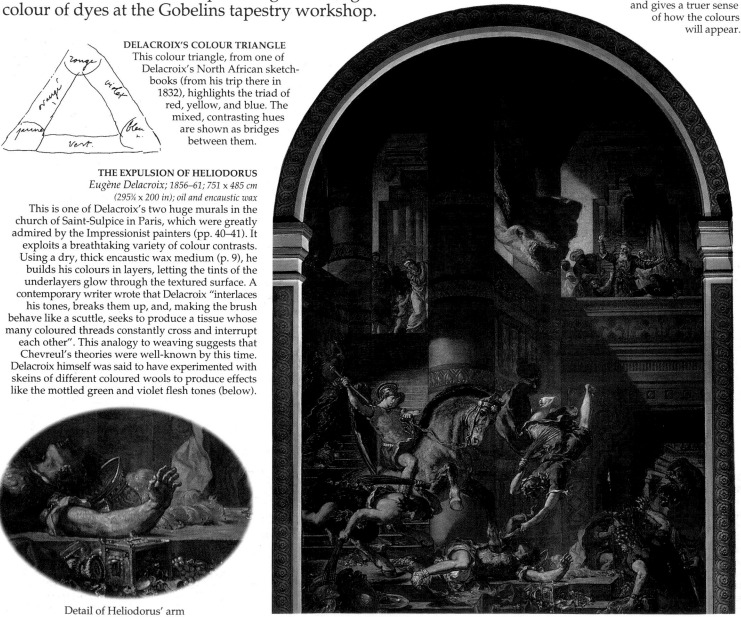

**DELACROIX'S PALETTE**
Delacroix used this extensive palette of luminous tones for his Saint-Sulpice mural (below). The light material of the palette, as opposed to traditional brown wood (which matched the brownish-red grounds of panel paintings), echoes the light ground of the painting, and gives a truer sense of how the colours will appear.

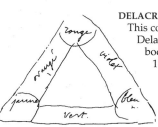

**DELACROIX'S COLOUR TRIANGLE**
This colour triangle, from one of Delacroix's North African sketch-books (from his trip there in 1832), highlights the triad of red, yellow, and blue. The mixed, contrasting hues are shown as bridges between them.

**THE EXPULSION OF HELIODORUS**
*Eugène Delacroix; 1856–61; 751 x 485 cm (295¼ x 200 in); oil and encaustic wax*
This is one of Delacroix's two huge murals in the church of Saint-Sulpice in Paris, which were greatly admired by the Impressionist painters (pp. 40–41). It exploits a breathtaking variety of colour contrasts. Using a dry, thick encaustic wax medium (p. 9), he builds his colours in layers, letting the tints of the underlayers glow through the textured surface. A contemporary writer wrote that Delacroix "interlaces his tones, breaks them up, and, making the brush behave like a scuttle, seeks to produce a tissue whose many coloured threads constantly cross and interrupt each other". This analogy to weaving suggests that Chevreul's theories were well-known by this time. Delacroix himself was said to have experimented with skeins of different coloured wools to produce effects like the mottled green and violet flesh tones (below).

Detail of Heliodorus' arm

# Chevreul's law of contrasts

In 1839, Chevreul published his book, "On the Harmony and Contrast of Colours". While working as Director of Dyeing at the Gobelins works, he had noticed that the brightness of colours did not depend only on the strength of the dyes. Some colours lost their intensity when they were placed next to each other, and from this he developed the simple "law of simultaneous contrast", as to which combinations of colours should be avoided, and which arrangements best enhance the purity or forcefulness of hues.

### CHEVREUL'S COLOUR WHEEL
To demonstrate his theories, Chevreul created a colour wheel (1861), in which 1440 dyes are derived from 12 principle colours. It provides a precise system of colour measurement, with 20 "degrees" of gradation, from brightness (white at the centre) to darkness (at the edges). Complementary colours are shown opposite each other.

The chemist Michel Eugène Chevreul

### COMPLEMENTARY COLOURS
Chevreul realized that maximum colour contrast could be achieved by placing certain colours side by side. If two colours are placed next to each other, the difference between them appears at its greatest ("simultaneous contrast"), but the effect is most marked when colours are "complementary". He defined the complementary of a hue as the colour of the portion of the spectrum it absorbed – for example, red mostly absorbs green. In painter's terms, these complementary pairs are yellow/violet, blue/orange, and red/green (above).

### ON ENGLISH COASTS (STRAYED SHEEP)
*William Holman Hunt; 1852; 43.2 x 58.4 cm (17 x 23 in); oil on canvas*
When this work, by the English Pre-Raphaelite artist William Holman Hunt, was exhibited in Paris in 1856, Delacroix noted, with amazement, "Hunt's sheep". A critic marvelled at how "Hunt made a colour speak, which, before him, had only slumbered." The sunlit coats of the sheep (detail, right) are tinged with the complementary colours that Goethe had observed in a snowy landscape: "During the day, owing to the yellowish hues of snow, shadows tending to violet have been observable ... as the sun set, and its rays diffused a most beautiful red colour ... the shadow colour turned to green."

### NEW PURPLES
At the time when Holman Hunt and Delacroix were brightening their palettes, vivid new colours were being developed (p. 40). Of these, the most famous was the first synthetic dye, "Perkin's mauve" (above), made from a distillation of coal tar. It was discovered by an English chemist in 1856.

# Impressions of nature

THE IMPRESSIONIST PAINTERS revolutionized colour by surrendering themselves to visual experience and mostly working directly from nature. Claude Monet (1840–1926) wrote: "When you go out to paint, try to forget what objects you have before you, a tree, a house, a field, whatever. Merely think: here is a little square of blue, here an oblong of pink, here a streak of yellow, and paint it just as it looks to you ... until it gives your own naïve impression of the scene before you." The attempt to capture nature's "impressions" was never, however, really this "naïve". Both Monet and Auguste Renoir (1841–1919) limited their palettes to pure, bright colours, using complementary hues – such as yellow and violet or red and green (p. 39) – to depict the vibration of light and atmosphere. They also used patches or brushstrokes of colour to create dazzling, mobile combinations that skilfully evoke fleeting weather conditions and sparkling sunlight.

**PAINTING IN THE OPEN AIR**
The well-known 19th-century caricaturist Honoré Daumier sketched this amusing cartoon of "Landscapists at Work" (1862) – suggesting one of the reasons why painting out of doors was so popular! The Impressionist artists believed that working out in the open air gave their pictures a freshness and sincerity.

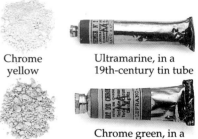

Chrome yellow

Ultramarine, in a 19th-century tin tube

Cadmium yellow

Chrome green, in a 19th-century tin tube

**NEW INVENTIONS**
The liberation of colour was aided by technological innovation. New, vibrant colours came into circulation, based on metallic chromium (c.1815) and cadmium (1820s). Later, the invention of collapsible tin paint-tubes (replacing pigs' bladders) made paint much more portable.

**RENOIR'S PALETTE**
Renoir's handwritten note lists his radiant palette of colours, among them cobalt blue, ultramarine, vermilion, emerald green, chrome yellow, and madder lake (known as "laque de Garance"). The earth tones are few: Renoir comments that "yellow ochre ... and raw sienna are intermediate tones only, and can be omitted, since their equivalents can be made with other colours."

**BOATING ON THE SEINE**
*Auguste Renoir; c.1879; 71 x 92 cm (28 x 36¼ in); oil on canvas*
Renoir's brilliant, sunlit painting is a striking example of the Impressionists' use of complementary colour. The bright orange rowing skiff glides through a sparkling expanse of pure cobalt blue, each colour enhancing the character and intensity of the other. The touches of vermilion, in one of the girl's dresses and in the reflections around the hull, heighten the vibration of the orange further. These effects faithfully record the way the colours actually appear: the eye experiences an after-sensation (p. 45) of orange after gazing at dazzling blue.

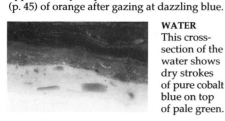

**WATER**
This cross-section of the water shows dry strokes of pure cobalt blue on top of pale green.

**RUSHES**
The rushes are painted in viridian, a chromium-based green, worked over chrome yellow.

# Woman with a Parasol

CLAUDE MONET *1875; 100 x 81 cm (39½ x 32 in); oil on canvas*
This wonderfully atmospheric painting of Monet's wife Camille and their son, Jean, features the violet-blue shadows that Monet loved. His wife stands on the crest of a hill, silhouetted against the sunlight. Her white dress is suffused with pale violet shadow and swathed in creamy yellow highlights, with little green tints dancing on to it from the grass. "I have at last discovered the true colour of the atmosphere," Monet later said, "It is violet. Fresh air is violet."

**MONET'S PALETTE**
During the 1860s, Monet turned his back on the dark colours that were associated with traditional Old Master techniques, and began to use pure, bright pigments. His palette from this period is dominated by the primary colours, whose importance had been stressed by Delacroix (p. 38), with greens and the indispensable lead white.

# Poetic colour

*"To name an object is to suppress three-quarters of the enjoyment .... To suggest it, that is the dream ...."*

Stéphane Mallarmé (1891)

IN THE LATTER HALF of the 19th century, dissatisfaction arose with the naturalistic aims of the Impressionist painters. This led to a revived interest in art as the expression of emotional and decorative ideas, as well as sensual and spiritual experience. In this new climate, the dominant relationship between colour and design became the key to the appreciation of the painting. The viewer no longer had to interpret the picture as a faithful record of visual sensations, or look for complex literary meanings. Instead, like poetry, the picture became simply a "suggestion" or an "allusion" – Stéphane Mallarmé, a Symbolist poet, compared a painting by Paul Gauguin (1848–1903) to "a musical poem that dispenses with a libretto [words]". While artists were liberated by the bright palette of the Impressionists, they now emphasized the evocative power of colour; Gauguin, for example, used the rhythms of colour planes and lines to suggest the heady atmosphere of the Tahitian landscape.

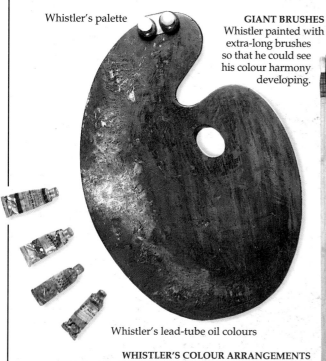

Whistler's palette

**GIANT BRUSHES**
Whistler painted with extra-long brushes so that he could see his colour harmony developing.

Whistler's lead-tube oil colours

**WHISTLER'S COLOUR ARRANGEMENTS**
Whistler's palette was carefully arranged to reflect the harmony of his predetermined colour scheme. Each hue was premixed, or adjusted on the canvas – but never mixed on the palette itself. White was placed at the top edge of the palette, with yellow to its left; then came siennas and umbers, blues, and, finally, reds and black. In contrast, Gauguin's palette (far right) shows traditional methods of mixing.

**THE WHITE GIRL (SYMPHONY IN WHITE, NO. 1)**
*James Abbott McNeill Whistler; 1862; 214.7 x 108 cm (84½ x 42½ in); oil on canvas*
The Anglo-American painter Whistler (1834–1903) described painting as "the poetry of sight", just as music was the "poetry of sound" (pp. 52–53). He believed that a picture should be appreciated first and foremost as an arrangement or "symphony" of colours and forms, and was exasperated by the public's attempts to discover a hidden literary or symbolic meaning in *The White Girl*. As a result, he prefixed the original title with "Symphony in White, No. 1". The girl was painted in diffused light, so that her form flattens into broad areas of pale tone and hue. Her features, however, emerge strongly from the mass of dark auburn hair.

## LAUS VENERIS

*Edward Coley Burne-Jones; c.1873–78;*
*122 x 183 cm (48 x 72 in); oil on canvas*

The Victorian artist Edward Burne-Jones (1833–98) uses rich colour to describe the languid and oppressive nature of sensual love. The picture evokes Swinburne's poem of the same title, in which references to blood – "Her little chambers drip with flower-like red" – suggest love's bitter pleasures.

Stained-glass panels from the Morris Window

## STAINED GLASS

Burne-Jones produced outstanding stained-glass designs for the artist William Morris (1834–96), whose famous firm of "fine art workmen" was founded on the ideal of medieval craftsmanship. Both used two-dimensional colour and light (above) to convey the radiance and simplicity of early Christian piety.

## HOLY WOMEN AT THE TOMB

*Maurice Denis; 1894; 74 x 100 cm*
*(29¼ x 39½ in); oil on canvas*

The French painter Maurice Denis (1870–1943) believed that "... a picture – before being a war horse or a nude woman or an anecdote – is essentially a flat surface with colours assembled in a certain order." This explains the decorative quality of his work, but the colour symbolism is also influenced by Denis' devout religious feeling.

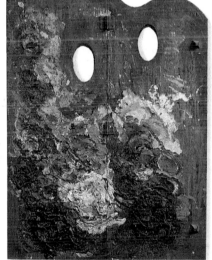

Gauguin's palette

## FATATA TE MITI (BY THE SEA)

*Paul Gauguin; 1892; 67.9 x 91.5 cm*
*(26¾ x 36 in); oil on canvas*

The Post-Impressionist painter Gauguin was inspired by the pulse and colour of life in Tahiti, and the example of Japanese prints (pp. 48–49), to create a vigorously individual ideal of colour harmony. He compared his colour arrangements to "oriental chants sung in a shrill voice, to the accompaniment of pulsating notes that intensify them by contrast". In this canvas, for example, he uses flat areas of lavender and mauve-pink for the earth. These unnatural colours are then intensified by the contrasting orange and yellow leaves.

43

# Colour science

T HE FRENCH NEO-IMPRESSIONIST painters
Georges Seurat (1859–91) and Paul Signac
(1863–1935) were the first to rigorously apply
19th-century scientific colour theories to
their works. Chevreul's ideas on colour
contrast (p. 39) were combined with the
discovery in the 1850s, by the Scottish
physicist James Clerk Maxwell, that colours
can be mixed "in the eye", as well as on the
palette. Maxwell had demonstrated this using revolving discs,
in which, for instance, spinning violet- and green-painted
segments produced the optical sensation of blue. In 1879, the
American artist and colour scientist Ogden Rood proposed
that identical optical effects "take place when different colours
are placed side by side in lines or dots, and then viewed at
such a distance that the blending is more or less accomplished
by the eye". This passage had an enormous influence on
Seurat, who began to juxtapose dots (French: "*points*") of
bright colour after 1882, systematically creating a technique
that became known as "*pointillism*" or "*divisionism*".

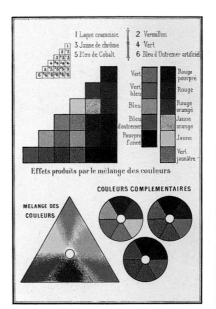

**SEURAT'S DOTS**
This three-times
magnification from
Seurat's *La Grand Jatte*
(below) shows minute
dots of colour. They
produce such a small
image on the retina
(p. 6) that their colour
does not always register.

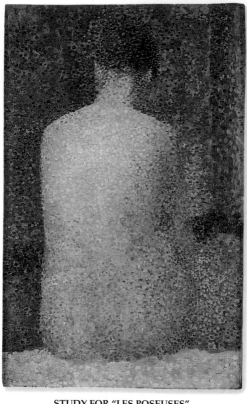

**STUDY FOR "LES POSEUSES"**
*Georges Seurat; 1887; 25 x 16 cm (9¾ x 6¼ in); oil on canvas*
This simple study of a nude shows Seurat using dots
of contrasting hues. These represent the interweaving
of natural flesh colours with the colours of light
(yellow and orange) and their complementary tints
of shadow (mauve and blue). The lightness of the
palette creates a gentle harmony of contrasts.

**ROOD'S "COLOURS AND APPLICATIONS"**
Rood accompanied his detailed discussion of the
difference between "optical mixtures" (mixtures in
the eye) and paint mixtures with colour triangles,
tables, and colour wheels (1881; frontispiece, left). His
proportions of light and colour were mathematically
measured to prove that optical mixtures could be as
luminous as the additive mixture of light (p. 7) – an
approach that appealed to the methodical Seurat.

**A SUNDAY AFTERNOON ON THE
ISLAND OF LA GRANDE JATTE**
*Georges Seurat; 1884; 207.6 x 308 cm
(81¾ x 121¼ in); oil on canvas*
Seurat made 23 preparatory drawings
and 38 oil studies for this painting alone.
There are no earth colours on the surface,
just pure tints, which he arranged on his
palette in the order of the spectrum. They
are used to create a mesh of colour,
echoing Rood's observation that grass
contains "yellowish-green, bluish-green,
reddish, purplish, and brown tints". These
hues "flicker and glimmer" close-up, but
at a distance they tend to appear dull.

# Portrait of Félix Fénéon in 1890

**PAUL SIGNAC** *1890; 73.9 x 93.1 cm (29 x 36¾ in); oil on enamel*

Here, Félix Fénéon, the critic who championed the art of Seurat and Signac, is flamboyantly depicted against a brilliant kaleidoscope of colour and curving line. Signac's portrait is influenced by Charles Henry's publication on the psychological, expressive effects of line and colour (right), which Fénéon had greeted as "a flowering, mathematical work of art that reanimates all the sciences." These interests are implied in the first part of the title: *Against the Enamel of a Background Rhythmic with Beats and Angles, Tones and Colours ....*

### JAPANESE INSPIRATION

The spiralling design in the background of Signac's portrait (detail, left) is adapted from a Japanese print that he owned. In one section, Signac has playfully juxtaposed yellow stars in a field of blue (suggesting the U.S. flag) with solar planets in a sky of pink.

### THE AFTER-IMAGE

This artwork illustrates the "after-image", an illusion described by Chevreul and analysed by Rood. To experience it for yourself, gaze at the green "spade" on the left for 15 seconds and then shift your attention to the spot on the right. You will see the "spade" appear again, but in its complementary colour – red (p. 39). The eye will normally avoid this after-sensation by moving continually.

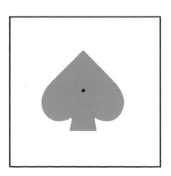

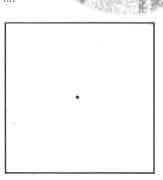

### COLOUR FROM NEW ANGLES

The scientist Charles Henry believed that warm and cold colours, together with the angle and direction of line, could be used to express "gaiety", "calmness", or "sadness". Artists could use his "Aesthetic Protractor" (above) to put these ideas into practice.

# A means of expression

THE DUTCH MASTER Vincent van Gogh (1853–90) and the Norwegian artist Edvard Munch (1863–1944) used colour in an exaggerated and distorted way to make powerful personal statements. "Instead of trying to reproduce exactly what I have before my eyes, I use colour more arbitrarily, so as to express myself more forcibly," wrote Van Gogh. He explained that if he was painting a fair-haired lady, he might choose "orange, chrome, or lemon colour" and make "a simple background out of the most intense and richest blue ...". The naturalism of the colours was of no concern to him: what mattered were the strong emotions that the colours aroused. Similarly, Munch used violent colour and disturbing linear rhythms to express his particular obsessions. Both men exerted a crucial influence on German Expressionist artists like Ernst Ludwig Kirchner (1880–1938), who jettisoned ideas of conventional colour harmony in favour of sharp, clashing colours that "reproduce the pure creative impulse".

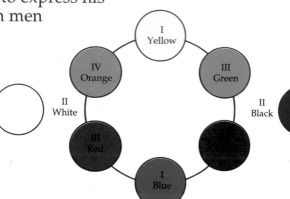

**GOETHE'S COLOUR TRIANGLE**
Goethe had already explored the effects of colour on the mind (pp. 36–37). His triangle divides the colours into four "mighty" hues (the four triangles at its apex), the "serene" colours (those in the left angle), and "melancholic" hues (those opposite). He felt their full impact could only be experienced if the eye was "entirely surrounded by one colour".

**THE COLOURS OF "ESSENTIAL" FEELING**
The Russian artist Wassily Kandinsky (pp. 52–53) believed that colour was the most effective means of communicating feeling. He represented his ideas about the spiritual and emotional power of colour in a rotating circle, "like a serpent biting its own tail". Black and white – "the two great possibilities of silence, death and birth" – float outside. The colours within the circle are paired in hot and cold combinations, with yellow, for instance, "the typical earthly colour", contrasting with "the heavenly colour" blue. "Morbid" violet partners "powerful" orange, while "determined" red is matched with "self-satisfied" green.

> **"**I have tried to express the terrible passions of humanity by means of red and green. **"**
>
> Van Gogh on *The Night Café*

**· THE NIGHT CAFE**
*Vincent van Gogh; 1888; 72.5 x 92 cm (28½ x 36¼ in); oil on canvas*
In this famous painting, Van Gogh has exploited the "clash and contrast of the most alien reds and greens" to express intense human alienation. He had admired the use of these complementary colours (p. 39) in a Delacroix painting, where "blood red" and "terrifying emerald" had been used to dramatic effect. Here, the emerald green ceiling and red walls, lit by the luminous yellow-green lamps, seem to press in on the figures slumped over the tables. Van Gogh also realized that the same hues could be used to express harmony and affection. Love between a couple, he imagined, could be movingly portrayed by the "marriage of two complementary colours" with their "mutual completion" and "vibration".

Edvard Munch on *The Scream*

**WOMEN ON THE SHORE**
In his graphic work, Munch investigated the power that colour has over mood and meaning. These two woodcuts are part of a set of six that were printed over a 30-year period. The earliest version (top), made in 1898, shows an old woman and a girl standing on a green shore, against a blue sky. Several colour variations later, the final print of the 1920s shows the girl's orange hair intensified to blood red, while the deeper black of the old woman subtly transforms her into a figure of death.

**THE SCREAM**
*Edvard Munch; 1893; 91 x 73.5 cm (35¾ x 29 in); oil, pastel, and casein on cardboard*
This jarring image is part of Munch's "Frieze of Life", an extraordinary cycle of paintings based on the subjects of "love and death". The artist explained that *The Scream* was inspired by a walk he was taking along the coastal path at sunset. In his tired and ill state, the clouds seemed to turn to blood red, and all of the colours of nature seemed to shriek. These harrowing effects are conveyed through violent, raw colour and swirling linear shockwaves. The "scream" seems to rush towards the viewer along the diagonal lines of the distorted perspective, invading the senses through dizzying contrasts of red and mauve. This combination of colours is intended to hurt the eye in the same way as a shrill cry pierces the ear.

**DRESDEN HOUSES**
*Ernst Ludwig Kirchner; 1909–10; 56 x 90 cm (22 x 35½ in); oil on canvas*
Kirchner's discordant colours disobey all the rules of colour harmony. The opposite effect – "clash", where colours react violently with one another – may be less serene, but the acidic colour combinations of pink, orange, red, yellow, blue, and green vividly give shape to Kirchner's immediate response to the scene. There is no regard for reality: areas of strident colour are bound by outlines in contrasting hues, and the white ground of the canvas is left visible.

# Patterns of the East

THE JAPANESE CONTRIBUTIONS to the International Exhibitions, held in London in 1862, and in Paris in 1876, 1878, and 1889, had an enormous impact on Western approaches to colour, composition, and design. Artists as diverse as the French Post-Impressionist painters Paul Gauguin and Pierre Bonnard (1867–1947), the Viennese Gustav Klimt (1862–1918), and the American-born James Whistler began to collect Japanese woodcuts and artefacts. They seized on the new potential of pattern, which was both decorative and abstract, the asymmetrical arrangements, fascinating colour combinations, and the striking balance of fine detail with large ambiguous expanses of colour. For Van Gogh in particular, the experience of "the brightly coloured Japanese prints that one sees everywhere" was overwhelming (the heightened colour of 19th-century woodcuts reflect the influence of the West). He began, in his own words, "to see things with an eye more Japanese, [to] feel colour differently".

**THE JAPANESE COLOUR SYSTEM**
The classical Japanese colour system differed from the West in having five "parent" (primary) colours: red, yellow, blue, black, and white (above). These were mixed to produce nine secondary colours: green, dark blue, sky blue, purple, dark green, orange, brown, and grey. A parent colour was rarely used alongside a secondary that was produced from it.

**SKETCH FOR "THE BALCONY", NO. 8**
*James Abbott McNeill Whistler; 1867; 61 x 48.2 cm (24 x 19 in); oil on panel*
Whistler based this sketch on two woodcuts by Kiyonaga in his collection, one of which is shown below. The colouring centres on a favoured Japanese combination of peachy pinks and turquoise-blues, which are woven together throughout the picture. In 1868, Whistler wrote of this to Fantin-Latour, noting that the Japanese "never look for contrast; on the contrary, they're after repetition".

**THE FOURTH MONTH**
*Torii Kiyonaga; c.1790; woodcut*
This print by Kiyonaga (1752–1815) employs subtle harmonies of black, white, peach, and warm and cool greys. The watery tones appealed to Whistler; he diluted his paints heavily with petrol or turpentine to create similar washes of delicate colour.

**CATCHING FIREFLIES**
*Eishosai Choki; mid-1790s; woodcut*
Eishosai Choki (active 1760s to early 1800s) was admired for his wonderful colouring and startling compositional techniques. Here, a small range of colours is subtly repeated throughout the picture: the orange-red flowers, for instance, are picked up in the ribbons worn by the woman and child, and in the details of their fans. Colour is used to create a play of patterns across the surface, from the checks, stars, and floral prints on the kimonos, to the swirls of water and spikes of grass. The print is also dominated by three bands of colour: the pale hues of the foreground give way to a solid mass of green, and a large expanse of black (now faded), lit by fireflies.

## CARTOON FOR THE STOCLET FRIEZE (FULFILMENT)
*Gustav Klimt; 1905–9; 194 x 121 cm (76½ x 47¾ in); appliqué on paper*
Klimt collected Japanese kimonos and theatrical Noh costumes (like the one on the right), as well as woodcuts and hanging scrolls. In this working design for the Stoclet frieze, commissioned to decorate the dining-room in the house of an industrialist, he swamped his embracing figures in voluptuous robes and locked them within the spiralling patterned background. The irregular areas of gold, black, and silver stand out from the ornamented surface of the man's costume like appliqué patch-work, mingling with a profusion of brightly coloured motifs.

A silk Noh costume, decorated with maple leaves on a chequered blue and gold background

### JAPANESE PATTERNING
The exquisite decoration of Noh costumes influenced a number of Western artists. The exotic combination of colours – turquoise with coral, for instance – was inspirational, as in Whistler's sketch (far left). In the asymmetrical patterning, rich, saturated patches of colour are scattered amid small, ornamental details.

### JAPANESE FOLDING SCREEN
In this 18th-century Japanese screen, gold is used to create a floating space that is filled with non-directional light. Gold was regarded in the East as the only "true" colour, because its shimmering surface suggested rather than defined. Such suggestive colour areas influenced the move away from realism in the West.

### PERE TANGUY
*Vincent van Gogh; 1887–88;*
*65 x 51 cm (25½ x 20 in); oil on canvas*
Van Gogh formed a collection of over 400 Japanese woodcuts, buying many from the art dealer and colour merchant Père Tanguy. Here, he has set Tanguy against a background of 19th-century coloured Japanese prints by his favourite artists, Hiroshige and Kunisada, in a pattern of blacks, reds, yellows, and greens.

In Japanese fashion, Bonnard's brightest colours move across his screen diagonally

### STREET SCENE
*Pierre Bonnard; 1899; each panel: 143 x 46 cm (56¼ x 18 in); coloured lithographs*
Bonnard combined the Japanese screen format with graphic techniques, to give his pictures a new type of decorative and spatial dimension. His four-panelled screen is hung with coloured lithographs, in which the spareness of detail is balanced against the expansive, "empty" background. The carriages at the top form a unifying band, although they are in the distance: space is suggested by what is known as "vertical" perspective – the higher up on the panel, the further away an object is.

# Picasso's changing palette

T HE SPANISH GENIUS PABLO PICASSO
(1881–1973) devoted his exceptionally long
career to exploring endless styles and themes.
Colour was one of his most versatile tools,
ranging from the chilly blues of his "Blue
Period" paintings – so-called because of their
overall colour and the sadness of their mood
– to the playful, strident colours of some of his
later works. During his Cubist phase, Picasso
became preoccupied with line and form, which
were traditionally associated with the intellect,
and colour, linked to the emotions, was virtually
eliminated. Subsequently, however, Picasso
moved happily between black and white and
colour, often producing variations on the same
theme in a spirit of exuberant experimentation.

**PICASSO IN HIS STUDIO**
Picasso surrounded himself with paints,
rags, pots, and tins, so that everything was
easily to hand. He squatted by his canvas,
which was often low down on the easel,
mixing his colours by leaning over
a table or kneeling on the floor.

**NOCTURNAL LIGHTING**
Picasso preferred to paint at night, by the
muted light of an oil lamp. In his early career he
sometimes could not afford the paraffin fuel, which
he also used as paint medium: one of his first blue
paintings was executed with a paintbrush in one
hand and a candle in the other. This weak light
made his indigo blues appear even more intense.

**THE TRAGEDY**
*Pablo Picasso; 1903; 105.4 x 69 cm (41½ x 27¼ in); oil on panel*
Picasso began "blue" painting in 1901, at the age of 20, as a morbid reaction
to a friend's suicide: "I began to paint in blue, when I realized Casagemas
had died." The artist was well aware of the colour's associations; Symbolist
painters in the 1890s had fallen in love with blue's "languid melancholy".
In Picasso's own mind, blue was the colour of sadness, cold nights, and
solitude, and it is no coincidence that his own circumstances were bleak
at this time. *The Tragedy*, painted in Barcelona in the winter of 1903, shows
a ragged family, barefoot and blue with cold, by the icy blue waters of
the sea. Their stark poverty suggests their alienation from society.

**MADAME CAMUS**
*Edgar Degas; c.1869–70; 72.7 x 92.1 cm (28½ x 36¼ in); oil on canvas*
The rich orange-reds of this portrait, by the Impressionist painter Edgar
Degas (1834–1917), form a stark contrast to Picasso's cool blues. Here, the
colour suggests the warmth and comfort of an intimate interior; Degas
was fascinated by the effects of artificial light. Picasso was to adopt
warmer colouring directly after his Blue Period, perhaps as a reflection
of his happier circumstances, or simply because he was tired of blue. It
has been suggested that the tender rose colouring of Picasso's pictures of
1905–7 (the "Rose Period") was influenced by his use of the drug opium.

**NUDE WOMAN**
*Pablo Picasso; 1910; 187.3 x 61 cm (73¾ x 24 in); oil on linen*
This work is a key painting of the brief phase (to 1912)
known as "Analytical" Cubism. In this style, developed
by Picasso and Georges Braque, space and forms were
analysed, disintegrated, and reassembled until they were
almost unrecognizable, while colours were remorselessly
reduced to black, white, brown, and grey. These are the
colours of spatial planes, voids, and edges, where darkness
is contrasted with brightness to suggest fragmented forms.

**HOUSES IN PROVENCE**
*Paul Cézanne; c.1880; 65 x 81.3 cm (25½ x 32 in); oil on canvas*
Picasso's Cubist paintings draw upon the
architectural logic of landscapes by Paul Cézanne
(1839–1906). Cézanne set square masses of cool
colour against warm colour, bright colour against
greyed colour, to create light, shade, and, above
all, a sense of structure. "Where colour has its
richness, form has its fullness," he once stated.

**LAS MENINAS ("THE MAIDS OF HONOUR")**
*Diego Velázquez; 1656; 318 x 276 cm*
*(125 x 108½ in); oil on canvas*
Throughout his career, Picasso was drawn to the
colour harmonies of his great Spanish predecessor,
Diego Velázquez (1599–1660). When a friend
commented on the "Spanishness" of Picasso's tans,
blacks, browns, and whites, which characterize
his Cubist paintings and his studio interiors of the
1950s, Picasso replied, "Velázquez". He based a
series of paintings directly on *Las Meninas* (below).

**LAS MENINAS: THE INFANTA
MARGUERITA MARIA, NO. 27**
*Pablo Picasso; 14 September 1957;
100 x 81 cm (39½ x 32 in); oil on canvas*
The Infanta is based on the little
Spanish princess at the centre of
Velázquez's *Las Meninas* (above).
Picasso had set up a huge, enlarged
black and white photograph of
Velázquez's picture in his studio
in 1957, and then devoted most of
the next five months to painting 44
variations on it, dating each picture
precisely. Some of his pictures include
the whole composition, in shades of
black and white, while others pull it
apart, and colour it with extraordinary
inventiveness. Here, Picasso has
depicted the Infanta turned towards
us so that most of her face is in dark
green and violet-blue shadow. Picasso
may have been aware that if neutral
colours, such as those in *Las Meninas*
(above), are stared at, after-images of
their complementary appear (p. 45),
producing an illusion of colour.

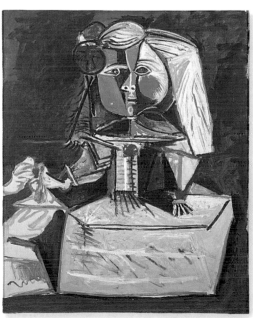

# Colour and music

**A MUSICAL COLOUR WHEEL**
Newton formed his seven colours of the spectrum (p. 6) into a colour circle, matching each rainbow hue to a portion of the musical scale.

**MUSICAL VIBRATIONS**
In the 17th and 18th centuries, the coloured wavelengths of light (p. 6) were thought to behave like the trembling vibrations of sound in a bell or the string of a lute. Artists imitated these by using ringing colour combinations.

THE LINK BETWEEN COLOUR AND MUSIC, the "sensations" of the eye and the ear, reached a new significance in 20th-century art. "Colour," wrote the Russian artist Wassily Kandinsky (1866–1944), "is the keyboard, the eyes are the harmonies, the soul is the piano with many strings. The artist is the hand that plays, touching one key or another, to cause vibrations in the soul." This notion of musical and colour harmony stretches back across the centuries. The artist known as the Master of the Saint Lucy Legend used the beauty of shot colour to suggest the divine harmonies of 15th-century choral music, while the Renaissance Italians equated musical measures with mathematical balance and proportion. However, in the 20th century, artists like Paul Klee (pp. 54–55) and Kandinsky used colour in a highly theoretical and philosophical way – associating tone with timbre (the sound's character), hue with pitch (whether a sound is pitched high or low), and saturation with the volume of sound. Kandinsky even claimed that when he saw colour, he heard music: he spoke of the azure flute, the blue cello, and the bass echo of black.

**MARY, QUEEN OF HEAVEN**
*Master of the Saint Lucy Legend; c.1485/1500; 199.2 x 161.8 cm (78½ x 63¾ in); oil on panel*
In this panel, by the Flemish Master of the Saint Lucy Legend, the Assumption and Coronation of the Virgin (where Mary is raised up to Heaven and crowned) is accompanied by the glorious music of singing and playing angels. The spiritual harmony of their music is expressed through radiant chords of colour, which are carefully distributed among the angels' robes. Leonardo compared the harmonious proportions of painting to "many different voices joined together and singing simultaneously ... which gives such satisfaction to the sense of hearing that listeners remain spellbound with admiration, as if half-alive." At the time this altarpiece was painted, music was mainly sung, with instruments such as the lute, viol, and harp being used to multiply the vocal parts.

**ZACCOLINI'S COLOUR MUSIC**
In *"De Colori"* (Italian: "About Colour"), which was popular in 17th-century Roman artistic circles, Matteo Zaccolini created a type of colour-music to be used therapeutically – as in the tarantella dance. The tarantella rhythms were thought to cure the poisonous bite of the tarantula, and Zaccolini believed that colours, matched to the musical chords, could aid the process.

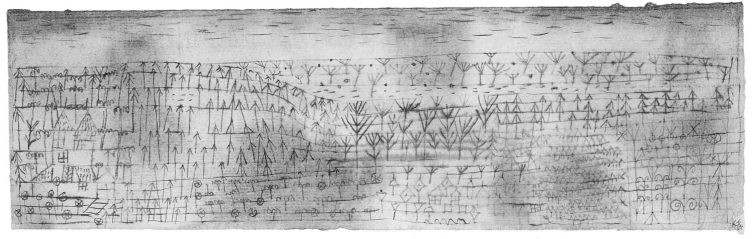

## JUNGER WALD (YOUNG FOREST)

*Paul Klee; 1925; 9.8 x 32.2 cm (3¾ x 12¾ in); pen and ink, and watercolour on paper, mounted on cardboard*

Klee came from an exceptionally musical family and was himself a very gifted violinist. He often incorporated musical theory into his pictures, using expressive colour and meticulous linear forms to create a harmonious synthesis of colour and line. Here, tiny arrows, bird's claws, and other suggestive shapes are the symbols of young trees and thickets, but they are arranged in horizontal bands as if they were hundreds of notes sitting on a musical stave. The fine pen lines mark out the musical rhythms and measures, and the hazy areas of colour are almost like the parts played by different instruments in an orchestra that enhance the overall richness of sound. Klee's fresh tints of rose, yellow, green, and blue also suggest growth and renewal.

## IMPROVISATION 31 (SEA BATTLE)

*Wassily Kandinsky; 1913; 140.7 x 119.7 cm (55½ x 47¼ in); oil on linen*

Kandinsky described his "improvisations" as "unconscious expressions of an inner impulse". Here, two battling sailing ships are just recognizable, but the painting is more concerned with Kandinsky's response to the idea of conflict. He has used colour – trumpeting yellows, loud and restless reds and oranges – to suggest the noise of battle, and isolated greens and blues to show the disruption of harmony.

### THE COMPOSER SCHÖNBERG

Many of Kandinsky's musical ideas were inspired by his close friendship with the composer Arnold Schönberg, who had broken away from traditional rules of musical composition. This photo of Schönberg, dated 12 December 1911, bears a cryptic message: "Dear Mr. Kandinsky, I free myself in notes from an obligation that I would have liked to fulfill long ago."

Ludwig Hirschfeld-Mack:
Color sonatina in red

### MUSIC IN THE KEY OF "RED"

The Bauhaus, a German school of craft and design, believed in bringing the arts together. Both Klee and Kandinsky taught there. This "Colour Sonatina in Red" was composed by one of its artists, Ludwig Hirschfeld-Mack, to accompany his coloured light compositions.

### THE SONG OF THE VOWELS

*Joan Miró; 1966; 366 x 114.8 cm (144 x 45¼ in); oil on canvas*

The Catalan artist Joan Miró (1893–1983) sought an abstract equivalent to musical ideas, using discs of colour. The "Song" of the title refers to a poem, "Vowels", by the French poet Rimbaud, in which colours are matched to vowels (A to black, E to white, I to red, O to blue, and U to green). Miró has varied the colour intensity, shape, and size of each disc, so that they seem to range from a full musical note to a tiny rhythmic accent.

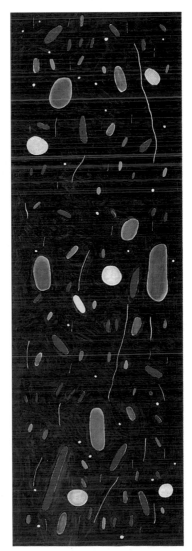

# Oriental light

IN APRIL 1914, THE SWISS ARTIST Paul Klee (1879–1940) set out for Tunisia in North Africa with his two painter friends, Auguste Macke (1887–1914) and Louis Moilliet. They went in the hope that, like Delacroix, Monet, Renoir, and Matisse before them, their art would be transformed by the revelation of oriental colour and light. Previously, Klee had worked mostly in black, white, and tonal greys, but as soon as he arrived he brought out his bright pots of watercolour. The pictures he painted in Tunisia, and in the years just after his return, are filled with delicate yellows, blues, mauves, greens, and the luminous white of the watercolour paper; later he used much more intense colours to conjure up the sun-flooded Tunisia of his memory. By the time he had reached his final destination, the ancient Arabic city of Kairouan, Klee had come to this euphoric realization: "Colour possesses me. I no longer have to pursue it. It will possess me always. I know it. This is the meaning of this happy hour: colour and I are one. I am a painter."

**THE CITY OF LIGHT**
On 15 April, Klee and his companions arrived at Kairouan, the "city of a hundred mosques". Their three-day stay had a profound effect on Klee. Here, he saw the colour theories of his Parisian friend, Robert Delaunay (p. 7), come to life: the architecture was shaped by pure colour and light, and the contrasting hues of sunlight and blue- and violet-tinged shadow vibrated with vitality.

**OUTSIDE THE GATES OF PARADISE**
This photo shows Klee and Macke (on the donkey) in 1914, outside the walls of Kairouan. The city was described in their 1911 Baedecker guide as one of the four gates to Paradise.

**AFRICAN INTRICACY**
The intricate patterns and colours of the Near East influenced Klee, just as they had Matisse (p. 57). This Moroccan textile, owned by Matisse, echoes the delicate lattice-work of the window grates in Morocco and Tunis. Klee often superimposed this patterning on his colours to give them a sense of rhythm (p. 53).

**KAIROUAN I**
*Auguste Macke; 1914; 21.4 x 27 cm (8½ x 10½ in); watercolour on paper*
Macke's watercolour of Kairouan at night explores the relationships between light and darkness, and warm and cool colour, which fascinated both him and Klee. The blue, cool colours divide the sky into strips, and the sands into patches of green, blue, and violet shadow; the warm colours, tending towards yellow, describe the glowing forms of the architecture and the heat that still radiates from the sands. Klee enthusiastically described their experience of an evening there as: "The essence of 'A Thousand and One Nights', which is, however, 99 per cent real. What an aroma, how penetrating, how intoxicating, and at the same time simple and clear."

1917 92.    Persische Nachtigallen.

# Persian Nightingales

**PAUL KLEE** *1917; 22.8 x 18.1 cm (9 x 7¼ in); gouache, watercolour, pen, ink, over graphite on paper*

This poetic picture was painted during the First World War, while Klee was on military service. His friends Macke and Franz Marc had been killed in action, and Klee spent much of his time in meditation. This watercolour combines the effect of his trip to Tunis with the influence of the classic Chinese poems in which he immersed himself. The delicate washes of colour are united with fine-line Arabic letters (R and N), interlaced with birds, moons, and stars. The colours are a "blond" echo of the "southern moon-rise" of Kairouan that had so inflamed Klee's soul.

**WATERCOLOUR MEDIUM**
The watercolour medium is perfect for capturing the radiance of light. Pigment is bound with a water-soluble medium, usually gum arabic from the acacia tree, and lighter tones are obtained by thinning with water. The watery glazes of colour are so translucent that the light from the paper shines through.

Portable watercolour box

**THE UNIVERSE IN MINIATURE**
Klee's combination of birds and blossoms resembles the designs of Persian tiles (right) and illuminations. He loved the hypnotic miniature patterns of these arts, because their natural detail evoked a whole "other" world of reality; a friend noted that Klee saw infinity in a green leaf or a butterfly wing. In the delicate colour balances, Klee also found confirmation of Cézanne's idea that colour is "the place where our spirits and the universe meet".

# Matisse's pure colour

"WHEN I PAINT GREEN, it doesn't mean grass; when I paint blue, it doesn't mean sky." In this way, the 20th-century master Henri Matisse (1869–1954) summed up the essence of his approach to colour. From the brilliant vigour of his early Fauvist paintings to the luminous serenity of his later masterpieces, Matisse freed colour once and for all from its literal, descriptive role – his choice of shades was governed by "observation", "feeling", and "the very nature of each experience". In order to match his colours to the intensity of his emotions, Matisse deliberately organized them in the most expressive way. If he needed a balance of pure, unmixed hues to provide a restful surface for the eye, he did not hesitate to create it. Often, he would change his colours while in the process of painting, until he achieved the harmonious combination of tones that he could already "see" in his mind's eye.

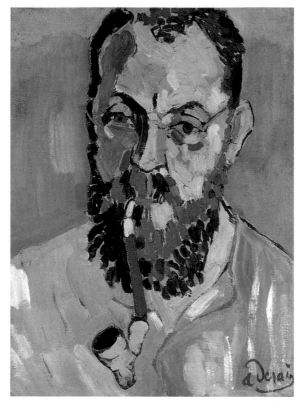

**HENRI MATISSE**
*André Derain; 1905; 46 x 34.9 cm (18⅛ x 13⅝ in); oil on canvas*
Derain painted this portrait of Matisse when they were both members of the "Fauves" (French: "wild beasts"). A critic had coined this unflattering name in response to the savage energy and fierce, unnaturalistic colour of their pictures (Matisse also wore a furry overcoat at the group's first exhibition!). The Fauves used vigorous daubs of paint, wielding colours like "sticks of dynamite". "We were always intoxicated with colour, with words that speak of colour, and with the sun that makes colours live," wrote Derain.

**AFRICAN INSPIRATION**
Matisse was among the first French artists to realize the power of African art. His fellow painters, André Derain (1880–1954) and Maurice de Vlaminck, stimulated by their visits to the primitive exhibits in the Paris Trocadéro, had begun to collect African masks and statuettes, and Matisse soon followed suit. (It was Matisse who introduced Picasso to African art.) The pure impulses of these artefacts inspired them to approach nature with the same directness and lack of prejudice.

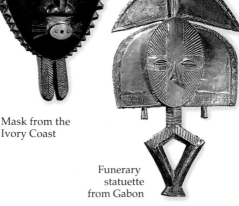

Mask from the Ivory Coast

Funerary statuette from Gabon

**HARMONY IN RED**
*Henri Matisse; 1908–9; 180 x 220 cm (71 x 86½ in); oil on canvas*
Here, Matisse has used colour of equal brightness and saturation throughout the picture, so that no area is seen to be the background. The figure, the table, the wall, the window, the lemons – all engage our attention equally, inviting our eye to move over the vibrating surface. The mutual attraction of these intense colours is similar to that of the Persian miniatures loved by Matisse (p. 27). But the huge expanse of red – with the red table flattening out to become unified with the red wall – flouts the rules of decorative harmony, in which bright patches of colour were usually small. He originally painted *Harmony in Red* in blue or blue-green, later altering the colour to create "a cocoon of warmth".

## THE LIGHT OF THE RIVIERA

From 1917, Matisse spent a great deal of his time in Nice on the French Riviera, making his home there in 1921. "When I realized that I would see that light every morning," he wrote, "I could not believe in my own happiness." Matisse's idol, Cézanne, had also lived and worked in this wonderful southern Mediterranean light: "The sunlight here is so intense," Cézanne noted, "that it seems to me that objects are silhouetted not only in black and white, but also in blue, red, brown, and violet ... this seems to me to be the opposite of modelling."

## CUTTING INTO COLOUR

Following two operations for duodenal cancer in 1941, Matisse was confined to a wheelchair. Undaunted by the fact that he could no longer paint at an easel, he began to make pictures out of pieces of cut-up coloured paper that had first been painted in gouache (the texture of the paint is clearly visible; right). "Cutting directly into colour," he wrote, "reminds me of the direct action of the sculptor carving stone." At last, he had found a form in which line (drawn by his scissors), colour, and idea could be realized simultaneously.

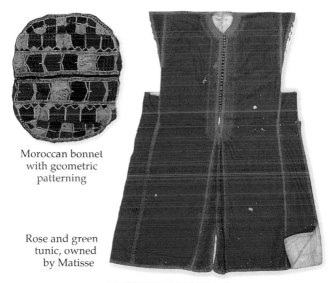

Moroccan bonnet with geometric patterning

Rose and green tunic, owned by Matisse

## OBJECTS FROM THE EAST

Throughout his life, Matisse drew inspiration from oriental cultures. He travelled to Algeria, Russia, Tangiers, and Polynesia, bringing back textiles (p. 54), costumes, and even seaweed and flowers. This Moroccan bonnet and tunic are two of the many beautiful items he surrounded himself with. From these – along with Persian miniatures, Russian icons, Islamic rugs, ceramics, and primitive sculptures – he learned about new colour harmonies and the rhythms of line.

## BEASTS OF THE SEA

*Henri Matisse; 1950; 295.5 x 154 cm (116¼ x 60½ in); paper collage on canvas*
This three-metre-high (eight-foot) canvas, filled with spiralling cut-out forms, recalls the artist's trip to Polynesia of 20 years earlier. It is based on Matisse's account of a "greyish-jade green lagoon" with pastel-tinted coral branches, "around which pass shoals of small fish, blue, yellow, and striped with brown .... And dotted about everywhere the dark brown of the sea cucumbers ...". His feelings for this watery paradise are re-created in clashing harmonies of mint, apple, and greyish-greens, pinks, purples, and mustard and lemon yellows. Recognizable shapes are stacked in blocks of colour, interlacing "like a cord or a serpent", as Matisse intended.

*les bêtes de la mer...*
*H. matisse 50*

# Abstract power

ABSTRACT ART – in which there are no recognizable references to the outside world – relies heavily on the dynamic nature of colour. By the early 20th century, photography had destroyed the documentary value of the realistic painted image, and artists were becoming increasingly interested in deepening and universalizing their sensations and ideas. For many, this meant a return to basics: the Dutch painter Piet Mondrian (1872–1944) used the relationships between lines and colours to bring into play "the whole sensual and intellectual register of the inner life". His cool, geometric abstraction contrasts with Kandinsky's expressive "improvisations" (p. 53). The emotive power of colour was realized most intensely in the all-enveloping canvases of the Russian-American artist Mark Rothko (1903–70), in which colour overwhelms the senses.

*"We all pay homage to clarity."*

Piet Mondrian, from his essay, "Plastic Art and Pure Plastic Art" (1945)

**WALL-HANGING IN RED AND GREEN**
*Gunta Stölz; 1926–27; 195 x 113 cm (76¾ x 44½ in); warp linen and weft cotton*
In the 1920s, Gunta Stölz (1897–1983) ran the weaving workshop at the influential Bauhaus school of design. This stunning wall-hanging closely reflects the teachings on colour of the Swiss painter and designer Johannes Itten, whose Bauhaus classes she attended. Itten believed that colour and form were inseparable – "Form and colour are one" – and that the simplest, most expressive elements were geometric shapes and the colours of the spectrum. He advised artists to exploit different kinds of colour contrasts, and to be sensitive to the emotional affinities between certain colours and certain shapes.

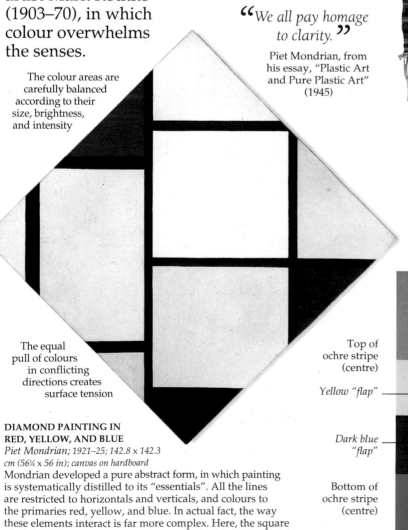

The colour areas are carefully balanced according to their size, brightness, and intensity

The equal pull of colours in conflicting directions creates surface tension

**DIAMOND PAINTING IN RED, YELLOW, AND BLUE**
*Piet Mondrian; 1921–25; 142.8 x 142.3 cm (56¼ x 56 in); canvas on hardboard*
Mondrian developed a pure abstract form, in which painting is systematically distilled to its "essentials". All the lines are restricted to horizontals and verticals, and colours to the primaries red, yellow, and blue. In actual fact, the way these elements interact is far more complex. Here, the square picture is presented in diamond format, which introduces the diagonal lines of the edges of the board. And in addition to the primaries, white, black, and grey set up new colour tensions.

Top of ochre stripe (centre)

*Yellow "flap"*

*Dark blue "flap"*

Bottom of ochre stripe (centre)

**REACTIONS BETWEEN COLOURS**
The artist Josef Albers (1888–1976) taught at the Bauhaus and became one of the most influential teachers of the 20th century. This cover from his book, "Interaction of Colour" (1974 edition), was specially designed to show that "colour has many faces". The dark blue and yellow strips of the original artwork were flaps that could be lifted to reveal an ochre stripe. The two small squares (top and bottom) are the tips of this stripe, and are the same colour! They only look different due to the surrounding hues.

# Red, Black, White on Yellow

**MARK ROTHKO** *1955; 266.7 x 236.2 cm (105 x 93 in); oil on canvas*

Rothko developed a severe and distinctive style, in which imposing canvases pulsated with large areas of colour. His pictures are often hung together in one room, so that the setting is filled with their mysterious resonance. "By saturating the room with the feeling of the work," Rothko wrote in 1954, "the walls are defeated, and the poignancy of each single work [is] more visible." The works are hung low, without frames, to ensure that the viewer experiences the drama of colour directly.

**ENIGMATIC VAGUENESS**
Rothko used his colour almost like a stain. It seeps beyond its blurred "edges", as in this detail, and seems to hover above the picture surface. The thin, brown ground of the canvas glows through the tones, giving them a strange, lurid quality. Unhappily, Rothko often used experimental materials and impermanent organic colours (p. 62). Now, many of his paintings are literally fading away.

**IKB 79**
*Yves Klein; 1959; 139.7 x 119.7 x 3.2 cm (55 x 47 x 1¼ in); acrylic and photography on panel*
The French experimental artist Yves Klein (1928–62) set out to rid colour of its emotional associations, freeing it to exist as a work of art in its own right. The *IKB* of the title stands for "International Klein Blue", an exceptionally intense blue that the artist patented as his own invention. In the late 1950s, Klein painted a series of pictures filled with this one vibrant blue. For his 1960 exhibition, naked women were smeared with this colour and dragged across canvases on the floor.

**AS IF TO CELEBRATE, I DISCOVERED A MOUNTAIN BLOOMING WITH RED FLOWERS**
*Anish Kapoor; 1981; wood, cement, polystyrene, pigment*
This sculpture, by the Indian-born artist Anish Kapoor (b.1954), uses vivid red and yellow powdered pigments of the type associated with Hindu worship. "The act of putting pigment on these objects removes all traces of the hand," he explains. "They are not made, they are just there."

Loose, pure colour gives the forms a ritualistic significance

# Fresh approaches

I**N THE POST-WAR PERIOD**, artists began to divorce colour from its traditional contexts. American painters, like Jackson Pollock (1912–56), started to apply colours in unusually direct and unconventional ways: paints – household emulsions, enamels, aluminium – were poured or splattered on to the canvas, with little intervention from traditional painting tools. For Pop artists (so-called because they borrowed images from popular culture), Pollock's thick, "scribbled" paint still smacked of painterly brushwork. Andy Warhol (1928?–87) reacted by embracing new mechanical techniques, like silk-screen printing, and synthetic colours and mediums: his *Green Marilyn* uses fluorescent paints, overprinted with a photographic image, to suggest a machine-made object. While Warhol's paints were still mostly brushed by hand, Morris Louis (1912–62) dripped his thinned acrylic paints over raw, unprepared canvas. Colour was finally freed from the distractions of surface texture and subject matter.

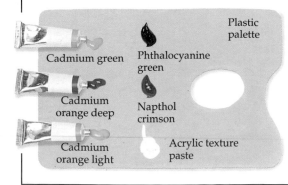

**GREEN MARILYN**
*Andy Warhol; 1964; 50.8 x 40.6 cm (20 x 16 in);*
*silk screen on synthetic polymer paint on canvas*
Warhol used gaudy colour to make images that were mass-produced – here, a publicity photo of Marilyn Monroe – more provocative and artificially appealing. The silk-screen method was borrowed from the world of commercial fabric printing.

**SUMMERTIME NO. 9A**
*Jackson Pollock; 1948; 84.8 x 555 cm (33½ x 218½ in); oil and enamel on canvas*
Pollock's famous "drip and splash" style dates from 1947. It involved dribbling paint from a dried-out brush or a can on to a huge canvas – here, areas in the squiggles of black enamel paint have been filled in with primary colours. In this way, Pollock hoped to achieve a direct expression of his unconscious moods. The technique was inspired by Indian sand-painting, in which coloured sands were trickled over one another. The texture of Pollock's pigments was all-important: he sometimes added sand or broken glass to create heavy *impasto*, working the paint with sticks, trowels, or knives.

Aluminium powder, used by Pollock in many works

**THE ACRYLIC MEDIUM**
Acrylic paint is pigment bound with a synthetic (plastic) resin. It dries quickly, and can be mixed with more resin or water to create different types of surface finish. It is ideal for creating flat, hard-edged colours, but it can also be used in thin washes. Acrylic ranges include many specially developed chemical colours, and texture paste for building *impasto* (left).

Plastic palette

Cadmium green

Phthalocyanine green

Cadmium orange deep

Napthol crimson

Cadmium orange light

Acrylic texture paste

**PEOPLE, BIRDS, AND SUN**
*Karel Appel; 1954; 173 x 242.8 cm (68 x 95½ in); oil on canvas*
Many modern artists continued to use traditional techniques in an individual way. The Dutch artist Karel Appel (b.1921) applies his strong oil colours thickly and crudely to re-create the spontaneous imagery of his inner world. Paints, however, are always mixed, and never used straight from the tube.

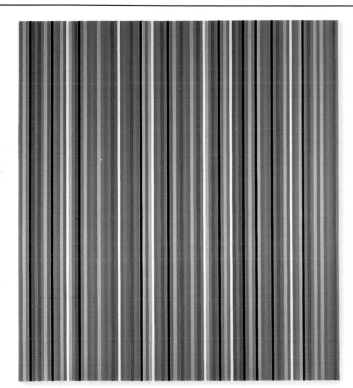

## LUXOR
*Bridget Riley; 1982; 223.5 x 197.5 cm*
*(88 x 77¾ in); oil on linen*

In her early colour works, the British artist Bridget Riley (b.1931) exploited the flicker and vibration of curves and spirals. She soon decided, however, that "colour energies need a virtually neutral vehicle if they are to develop uninhibited". Here, Riley has used plain vertical stripes in a limited palette inspired by Egyptian tomb paintings (below). The hues – echoing the desert, earth, water, sky, and greenery – interact with one another to generate their own space, colours, and light, while also retaining their individual intensity.

A photograph, owned by Riley, of a tomb painting from Luxor

Riley analysing colour combinations

### MIXING COLOURS
Bridget Riley works in a meticulous way, carefully mixing her colours to achieve the exact hue and intensity desired. Colour interaction is initially explored in small gouache colour studies, moving on to full-size paper-and-gouache designs (as in the photograph above). The large-scale canvas is then measured up and painted entirely by hand – first in acrylics, and then in oil.

## ALPHA-PHI
*Morris Louis; 1961; 259.1 x 459.1 cm*
*(102 x 180¾ in); acrylic on canvas*

The American painter Morris Louis developed an innovative method that gave an independent life to colour. He poured thinned Magna acrylic paint (one of the new ranges) on to unprimed cotton canvas, so that the colour soaked into the weave. In oil painting, the canvas must be primed (covered with a preparatory layer or ground) to prevent an oil, such as linseed, from destroying the fibres of the cloth. Acrylic allowed Louis to eliminate this barrier, so that the surface of the canvas seems to be stained with colour. *Alpha-Phi* is just one of a series of paintings, entitled "Unfurleds", in which this technique is used to breathtaking effect. The liquid colour flows sensuously across the lower corners, bounding the vast, empty space in-between. The effect is one of pure liquid colour, rather than of paint applied manually to a surface.

# Glossary

**"Additive" primaries** The three primaries of coloured light (orange-red, green, and blue-violet), from which all other colours can be mixed. These are different to the primaries of pigments, inks, and photographic emulsions ("subtractive" primaries).

**"Additive" mixing** The combining or "adding together" of the additive primaries, to create other coloured lights.

**Aerial perspective** A colouristic effect, used in landscape backgrounds, in which colours are painted paler and bluer the further they appear from the eye. This imitates colours in nature: blue light is scattered by the moist air of the intervening atmosphere.

**After-image** The image which remains after we stare fixedly at a colour and then shift our gaze to a plain white or neutral surface. This "negative" image is the original colour's "complementary" (below). This occurs because the eye tires quickly when it looks at one colour intensely, and, for a moment, can only see the colour that dominates the remainder of the spectrum.

**Azurite** A mineral pigment (copper carbonate): blue/blue-green.

Egg, used in tempera painting

**Brilliant colours** Colours of high intensity and purity.

**Broken colour** Mixed or tertiary colour.

**Cadmium colours** Opaque pigments based on sulphides of the element cadmium.

*Cangiante* (Italian: "changing") A type of colouring that imitates shot silk, in which bright contrasting colours are alternated in highlight and shadow. Often used for the draperies of angels to create supernatural effects.

*Chiaroscuro* (Italian: "bright-dark") A type of colouring that uses extremes of light and shade to make illuminated forms appear three-dimensional. The contrasts are often used to give forms theatrical impact.

**Chromium colours** Opaque pigments based on compounds of the element chromium, such as

viridian (a strong, cold green) and chrome yellow. Mainly used from the early 19th century.

**Cobalt colours** Pigments based on compounds of the element cobalt; the first cobalt pigment, cobalt blue, was discovered in 1802.

**Complementary colour** The true contrast or "negative" colour of any given hue: the colour of the dominant wavelength that the hue absorbs is its complementary. When a colour is mixed with its complementary (physically and optically – see "optical mixing"), both hues are neutralized (to a grey-black). When they are placed side by side, they intensify each other by contrast (see "after-image" and "simultaneous contrast").

**Cool colours** Colours that tend towards blue, most obviously those in the blue-green-violet range. It has been shown that cool colours actually slow down the viewer's circulation, causing a slight drop in body temperature.

**Copper resinate** Transparent deep green glaze; verdigris (or other copper salt) in resin and oil.

**Earth colours** Natural pigments found in the ground, made up of iron oxides mixed with varying proportions of clay. The colours range from dull red, yellow, orange, and brown to black, and are found in the form of ochres, umbers, and siennas. Earth pigments can be burnt or roasted to produce warmer shades.

**Gesso** (Italian: "gypsum") A white plaster-like material, mixed with animal glue ("size"), for use as a preparatory layer ("ground") in early Italian panel painting.

**Glaze** Transparent paint.

**Ground** The preparatory surface for a painting.

**Hue** The apparent colour of a visual sensation, described as "red", "blue", and so on.

*Impasto* Paint applied in thick, raised brushstrokes.

**Lake pigment** A soluble dye, which is formed into solid particles by being deposited on a powdered base such as chalk or aluminium oxide. Lakes are usually translucent when mixed with a medium, and are ideal for glazes.

**Lead white** An opaque white pigment, produced synthetically.

**Local colour** Colour as it appears in nature (such as green for grass).

**Luminosity** Giving the appearance of conveying a large amount of light.

**Medium** A binding agent, like oil

or egg, which makes the particles of pigment stick together and also binds them to the prepared surface.

**Modelling** The building up of forms in lights and darks (to suggest light and shaded areas), to make them look three-dimensional.

**Neutral colours** "Colours" on the white-grey-black scale.

**Opaque** Unable to transmit light: not transparent. An opaque pigment has good hiding power (obscuring the ground or colour beneath it).

**Optical mixing** When colours are blended in the eye, rather than being physically mixed together.

**Organic pigments** Pigments of animal or plant origin (often unstable).

**Palette** Both the surface on which the painter lays out his colours, and the range of colours chosen.

**Pigment** The colouring matter (usually in the form of a powder) used in painting.

**Primary colours** The fundamental colours, which cannot be created by mixture, but which can be combined to create other colours. The purest primary colours of pigment are magenta (bluish-red), cyan (greenish-blue), and yellow (used in modern colour printing), which are more simply perceived as red, blue, and yellow.

**Priming** Preparing a surface (ground) for painting on.

**Resin** A sticky natural substance from plants or trees, used to make glazes and varnishes, or as a binding medium.

**Saturation** The depth or "colourfulness" of a colour, and its freedom from grey.

**Secondary colour** A colour made by mixing two primaries together.

*Sfumato* (Italian: "smoky") A type of colouring, which uses mid-range colours, in which the transitions between colours are softened and blurred to give a naturalistic misty appearance.

**Shot colour** *Cangiante* colouring (above) that imitates the different coloured threads in woven silk; these change from one hue to the next according to the angle of the light.

**Simultaneous contrast** The effect produced when contrasting or complementary colours are placed next to one another: the colours will appear heightened in intensity, and totally dissimilar to one another.

**Spectral colours** The constituent colours of white light.

**Stable pigments** Pigments which do not fade, or alter chemically, over time.

Complementary colours

**"Subtractive" mixing** The blending of pigments, in which colours absorb or "subtract" light. The resultant colour is provided by the dominant wavelength that is not absorbed by the pigment. When the three subtractive primaries are mixed, they produce grey-black.

**"Subtractive" primaries** The pure primaries used in modern colour printing: magenta, cyan, and yellow.

*Terra verde* (Italian: "green earth") A natural, dull green pigment, made from clay, containing the mineral glauconite or celadonite.

**Tertiary colour** A colour produced by mixing two secondaries.

**Tone** The degree of lightness or darkness of a colour.

Shot colour

**Ultramarine** An exceptionally pure blue pigment extracted from the lapis lazuli stone. Synthetic equivalent produced since c.1830.

**Undermodelling** The preliminary depiction of forms, in broad terms of light and shade, during the early stages of a painting.

**Verdigris** A copper-based green pigment, often mixed with resin to make the deep green glaze copper resinate.

**Vermilion** An opaque red pigment, made from the mineral cinnabar, and produced artificially (mercuric sulphide) from ancient times.

**Warm colours** Colours that tend towards yellow, most obviously those in the red-orange-yellow range. Warm colours stimulate the viewer's circulation and cause a slight rise in body temperature.

**Wavelength** The distance between two adjacent identical points on a light wave, which gives a spectral light its apparent colour quality.

Red ochre          Yellow ochre

# Featured works

## Look here to find the location of, and complete details about, the works featured in the book.

This section also includes photographic acknowledgements, although further information can be found under "Acknowledgements" (p. 64).

Every effort has been made to trace the copyright holders and we apologize in advance for any unintentional omissions. We would be pleased to insert the appropriate acknowledgement in any subsequent edition of this publication.

**Key:** *t*: top; *b*: bottom; *c*: centre; *l*: left; *r*: right

**Abbreviations:**
**AIC:** The Art Institute of Chicago, All Rights Reserved; **BAL:** Bridgeman Art Library; **BIF:** Bibliothèque de l'Institut de France, Paris; **BL:** By Permission of the British Library; **BM:** The Trustees of the British Museum, London; **BN:** Bibliothèque Nationale, Paris; **FC:** © Frick Collection, New York; **FW:** Fitzwilliam Museum, Cambridge, UK; **HA:** © Hunterian Art Gallery, University of Glasgow; **ML:** Musée du Louvre, Paris; **MO:** Musée d'Orsay, Paris; **NGL:** Reproduced by Courtesy of the Trustees of the National Gallery, London; **NGW:** © National Gallery of Art, Washington; **PC:** Private Collection; **SC:** Scala; **TG:** Tate Gallery, London; **V&A:** Courtesy of the Board of Trustees of the Victoria and Albert Museum, London

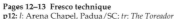

*Romano-Egyptian Funerary Portrait* (p. 9)

**Front cover:** clockwise from top left. Runge's colour sphere (p36); Harris' prismatic colour wheel (p36); Rose and green gandoura (p57); first plate of Goethe's "Theory of Colours" (p36); *The Night Café* (p46); gilding materials (p11); *The Wish of the Young St. Francis to Become a Soldier* (p15); *The Great One* (p9) **Inside front flap:** *b*: *The Coronation of the Virgin* (p14). **Back cover:** clockwise from top left: Florentine scales (p14); *The Toreador Fresco* (p12), *Light and Colour (Goethe's Theory)* (p37); Turner's paintbox (p37); *Ginevra de' Benci* (p20); Chalice of the Abbot Suger of St. Denis (p10); *The Court of Justinian* (detail, p10); *Maestà* (pp10–11); Goethe's colour triangle (p36); *The Adoration of the Magi* (p17); florins (p14); centre: *Fatata te Miti (By the Sea)* (p43)

**p1 (Half Title):** *The Adoration of the Magi* (p17); **p2:** *tl*: Stained glass windows in the Church of St. Peter and St. Paul (p43); *tc*: Rose and green gandoura (p57) *c*: *The Great One* (p9); *cr*: Persian illuminated manuscript, BM (p27); *bl*: Restored *Libyan Sibyl* (p28); *br*: *As if to Celebrate, I Discovered a Mountain Blooming with Red Flowers* (p59) **p3 (Title Page):** *tl*: Frontispiece of "Colours and Applications"(p44); *tr*, *cr*: Details of first plate of Goethe's "Theory of Colours" (p36); *c*, *bl*: *The Wish of the Young St. Francis to Become a Soldier* (p15) **p4:** *tl*: Atsuita Karaori kimono (p49); *cl*: *The Ascension of Mohammed* (p4); *cr*: Persian tiling (p55); *bc*: Theban brushes(p8); *br*: *Portrait of Félix Fénéon in 1890*, Paul Signac (p45)

David, *The Rest on the Flight Into Egypt* (p. 24)

**Pages 6–7 What is colour?**
**p6:** *c*, *b* (detail): *Study for a Portrait of Bonnard*, Edouard Vuillard, Musée du Petit Palais, Paris/Photothèque des Musées de la Ville de Paris/© DACS 1993 **p7:** *tc*: Printers' inks; *tr*: *Political Drama*, Robert Delaunay, NGW, Gift of Joseph H. Hazen Foundation, Inc/© ADAGP, Paris, and DACS, London 1993; *bl*, *c*: *Horse* (Red side and blue side), Alexander Calder, NGW, Gift of Mrs. Paul Mellon in Honour of the 50th Anniversary of the NGW/© ADAGP, Paris, and DACS, London 1993; *br*: *Runge's Colour Sphere Depicted as a Star*, Johannes Itten/© DACS 1993

**Pages 8–9 Ancient materials**
**p8:** *tl*: *Rotunda frieze*, Lascaux Caves, Caisse Nationale des Monuments Historiques et des Sites/© DACS 1993; *cr*: *Food for a Banquet*, Ardea, London; *bc*: Egyptian palette, BM **p9:** *t*: *Woman Being Flagellated and Dancing Bacchus*, Villa dei Misteri, Pompeii/SC; *bl*: Theban brushes, BM; *bcl*: *The Great One*, BM/Photo © Michael Holford; *br*: *Romano-Egyptian Funerary Portrait*, ML

**Pages 10–11 The splendour of gold**
**p10:** *tl*: Chalice of the Abbot Suger of St. Denis, © 1992 NGW, Widener Collection; *cl*, *tr* (detail): *The Court of Justinian*, San Vitale, Ravenna/SC; *bl*: *The Ascension of Mohammed* (from a Persian illuminated manuscript), BL **pp10–11** *b*, *tl*: *Maestà* (front), Duccio, Museo dell'Opera Metropolitana/SC **p11:** *tc*: Sicilian textile, V&A; *cr*: gilding materials

**Pages 12–13 Fresco technique**
**p12:** *l*: Arena Chapel, Padua/SC; *tr*: *The Toreador Fresco*, National Archaeological Museum, Athens/BAL; *cr*, *br* (detail): *Lamentation over the Dead Christ*, Giotto, Arena Chapel, Padua/SC **p13:** *c*, *br* (detail): *The Tribute Money*, Masaccio, Brancacci Chapel, Chiesa del Carmine, Florence/SC; *bl*: The King's Room, Würzburg Rezidenz, Würzburg/SC

**Pages 14–15 The value of colour**
**p14:** *tl* (detail): Early 12th-century treatise, Trinity College, Cambridge/BAL, *tr*: 17th-century Florentine scales, Science Museum, Florence/Photo: Franca Principe; *cr*: Florentine florins, BM; *b*: *The Coronation of the Virgin*, Enguerrand Quarton, Musée Pierre de Luxembourg, Villeneuve-Les-Avignon/Photo: Daspet **p15:** *c*, *cl* (detail): *The Kiss of Judas*, Giotto, Arena Chapel, Padua/SC; *t*, *cr* (detail): *The Wish of the Young St. Francis to Become a Soldier*, Sassetta, NGL; *br*, *bc* (detail): *The Crucifixion*, Masaccio, Museo di Capodimonte, Naples/SC

**Pages 16–17 Egg tempera painting**
**p16:** *tl*: Page of Cennino Cennini's "*Il Libro dell'Arte*", Biblioteca Medicea Laurenziana, Florence/Photo: Donato Pineider; *tr*: Back of panel, *Saint Paul*, Bernardo Daddi © 1993 NGW, Andrew W. Mellon Collection *b*: Three parts of an altarpiece: (*l*: *Adoring Saints*; *r*: *Adoring Saints*; *c*: *The Coronation of the Virgin*), Lorenzo Monaco, NGL **p17:** *tl*: *The Adoration of the Magi*, Fra Angelico and Filippo Lippi © 1993 NGW, Samuel H. Kress Collection; *tr*: "The Story of Thamyris", from Boccaccio's "De Claris Mulieribus", BN/BAL; *cl*: (detail) *Maestà* (front), Duccio, Museo dell'Opera Metropolitana/SC, *bl*: Paint cross-section (flesh of hand) from *David*, Santa Croce Altarpiece, Ugolino di Nerio, NGL; *br*: *Virgin and Child with St. Andrew and St. Peter*, Cima da Conegliano, National Gallery of Scotland, Edinburgh

**Pages 18–19 Colour, light, and narrative**
**p18:** *c*, *tl* (detail): *The Resurrected Christ*, Isenheim altarpiece, Grünewald, Musée d'Unterlinden, Colmar, France/Photo: O. Zimmermann; cl: *The Small Crucifixion*, Grünewald, © 1993 NGW, Samuel H. Kress Collection; *bl*: Engraving after a miniature from a 14th-century edition of St. Bridget of Sweden's "Revelations", Mary Evans Picture Library, London; *br*: *The Annunciation*, Piero della Francesca, San Francisco, Arezzo/SC **p19:** *l*, *br*: *Adoration of the Shepherds*, El Greco, Prado, Madrid/SC; *tr*: *The Alba Madonna*, Raphael, NGW, Andrew W. Mellon Collection

**Pages 20–21 Leonardo's naturalism**
**p20:** *tr*, *c*: Leonardo Manuscripts, The Royal Collection © 1993 H.M. Queen Elizabeth II; *br*, *bl* (detail): *Ginevra de' Benci*, Leonardo da Vinci, NGW, Ailsa Mellon Bruce Fund **p21:** *t*: *The Virgin, Infant Jesus, and St. Anne*, Leonardo da Vinci, ML/RMN; *bl*: Leonardo Manuscript, BIF

**Pages 22–23 Colouring in oils**
**p22:** *cl*: Illustration of madder plant, Winsor and Newton, Harrow, Middlesex; *r*, *bl* (paint analyses): *The Annunciation*, Jan van Eyck, NGW, Andrew W. Mellon Collection; **p23:** *tl*: *Tarquin and Lucretia*, Titian, FW; *tr* (paint analyses), *c* (X-ray): Hamilton Kerr Institute /FW; *br*, *bl* (detail), *Minerva Protects Pax from Mars (Peace and War)*, Rubens, NGL

**Pages 24–25 Colour and space**
**p24:** *tr*: *Paesaggio*, National Museum, Naples/SC; *cr*, *cl* (detail): *The Rest on the Flight Into Egypt*, Gerard David, NGW, Andrew W. Mellon Collection; *bl*, *br*: *Landscape with Hagar and the Angel*, Claude Lorrain, NGL **p25:** *t*: *The Dogana and Santa Maria della Salute, Venice*, J.M.W. Turner, NGW, Given in memory of Governor Alvan T. Fuller by the Fuller Foundation, Inc.; *b*, *c* (detail): *Wivenhoe Park, Essex*, John Constable, NGW, Widener Collection

**Pages 26–27 The Venetian School**
**p26** *tl*: Bird's-eye view of Venice, Jacopo de'Barbari, BM; *tr*: *Christ in Judgement and the Four Evangelists*, Pala d'Oro, San Marco, Venice/SC; *br*, *bl* (detail): *Danäe*, Titian, Museo del Prado, Madrid/SC **p27:** *t*: *The Family of Darius before Alexander*, Veronese, NGL; *cl*: Persian illuminated manuscript, BM; *c* (detail): *Tarquin and Lucretia*, Titian, FW; *br*: Medieval dyers, Colour Museum, Bradford, UK

**Pages 28–29 The restoration of colour**
**p28:** *tr* (detail): Eve's face, *Garden of Eden* (central ceiling panel; before restoration), Sistine Ceiling, Michelangelo, SC; *l*: *The Libyan Sybil* (after restoration), Sistine Ceiling, Michelangelo © Nippon Television Network Corporation 1993; *c*: *The Libyan Sybil* (before restoration), Sistine Ceiling, Michelangelo, SC; *br*: *The Feast of the Gods* (before restoration), Giovanni Bellini and Titian, NGW, Widener Collection **p29:** *t*, *br* (paint analyses): *The Feast of the Gods*, NGW, Widener Collection; *bc*: Florentine 16th-century Small Ewer, NGW, Widener Collection

Seurat, *A Sunday Afternoon on the Island of La Grande Jatte* (p. 44)

**Pages 30–31 Chiaroscuro: light and shadow**
**p30:** *tl*: Candle, Science Photo Library; *l*, *bl* (detail): *The Calling of St. Matthew*, Caravaggio, San Luigi dei Francesi, Rome/SC; *r*, *br* (detail): *The Repentant Magdalene*, Georges de La Tour, NGW, Ailsa Mellon Bruce Fund **p31:** *t*: *A Woman Bathing in a Stream*, Rembrandt, NGL; *cr*: *Rembrandt's Studio with a Model*, Rembrandt, Ashmolean Museum, Oxford; *br*: *Still Life with Melon and Peaches*, Edouard Manet, NGW, Gift of Eugene and Agnes E. Meyer

**Pages 32–33 Painting with light**
**p32:** *l*, *br* (detail): *The Girl with the Red Hat*, Jan Vermeer, NGW, Andrew W. Mellon Collection; *tr*: Room-type camera obscura, from Athanasius Kircher's "*Ars Magna Lucis et Umbrae*", Rome, 1649 **p33:** *t*: *A Lady Taking Tea*, Jean-Baptiste Chardin, HA; *bl*, *br* (detail): *Still Life*, Henri Fantin-Latour, NGW, Chester Dale Collection

**Pages 34–35 Rococo decoration**
**p34:** *l*: *Hollyhocks*, Jean-Honoré Fragonard, FC; *tr*: *Love As Conqueror*, Jean-Honoré Fragonard, NGW, In Memory of Kate Seney Simpson; *c*: View of the Boucher Room, FC; *bc*: Chinese jar and Sèvres vase, FC **p35:** *tl*: *A Young Girl Reading*, Jean-Honoré Fragonard, NGW, Gift of Mrs. Mellon Bruce in Memory of her Father, Andrew W. Mellon; *r*: *Hollyhocks*, Jean-Honoré Fragonard, FC; *c*: Gobelins tapestry, ML/RMN; *bl*: Gilt bronze tripod table, FC; *br*: "A Tintbook of Historical Colours Suitable for Decorative Work", John Oliver, London

**Pages 36–37 Goethe's colour theory**
**p36:** *tl*: First plate of Goethe's "Theory of Colours"; *l*: *Morning*, Philipp Otto Runge, Kunsthalle, Hamburg/Artothek; *cr*: Colour sphere, Philipp Otto Runge, Kunsthalle, Hamburg; *br*: Moses Harris' prismatic colour wheel, from "The Natural System of Colours", Royal Academy of Arts Library, London **p37:** *tl*: Diagram of Goethe and Newton's colour spectrums from Goethe's "Theory of Colours"; *cl*: Goethe's colour wheel from his "Theory of Colours"; *tr*: Title page of Charles Eastlake's translation of Goethe's "Theory of Colours", BL; *bl*: *Shade and Darkness, the Evening of the Deluge*, J.M.W. Turner, TG; *cr*: *Light and Colour (Goethe's Theory) – Morning after the Deluge – Moses Writing the Book of Genesis*, J.M.W. Turner, TG; *br*: Turner's paintbox, TG

**Pages 38–39 Harmony and contrast**
**p38:** *tr*: Delacroix's palette, V&A; *cl*: Delacroix's colour triangle, Musée Condé, Chantilly; *br*, *bl* (detail): *The Expulsion of Heliodorus from the Temple*, Eugène Delacroix, Saint-Sulpice, Paris/Lauros-Giraudon **p39:** *tl*: Chevreul's colour wheel, BN; *tc*: Photo of Chevreul, BN; *c*, *b* (detail): *Our English Coasts, (Strayed Sheep)*, William Holman Hunt, TG; *r*: Perkin's original mauveine, Colour Museum, Bradford, UK

**Pages 40–41 Impressions of nature**
**p40:** *l*: Renoir's list of colours, Document Archives Durand-Ruel, Paris; *br*, *bl* (paint analyses): *Boating on the Seine*, Auguste Renoir, NGL **p41:** *t*, *r* (detail): *Woman with a Parasol – Madame Monet and Her Son*, Claude Monet, NGW, Collection of Mr. and Mrs. Paul Mellon; *br*: Monet's palette, Musée Marmottan, Paris

**Pages 42–43 Poetic colour**
**p42:** *l*, *c*: Whistler's palette, paints, and brushes, HA, Birnie Philip Bequest; *r*: *The White Girl (Symphony in White, No. 1)*, James Abbott McNeill Whistler, NGW, Harris Whittemore Collection; **p43:** *tl*, *tc* (detail): Stained glass windows, south aisle of the Church of St. Peter and St. Paul, Cattistock, Reproduced by Courtesy of the Friends of Cattistock Church, Dorset; *tr*: *Laus Veneris*, Edward Coley Burne-Jones, Laing Art Gallery, Newcastle upon Tyne (Tyne and Wear Museums); *c*: *Holy Women at the Tomb*, Maurice Denis, Musée du Prieuré, Saint-Germain-en-Laye/Lauros-Giraudon, Paris/© DACS 1993; *bl*: *Fatata te Miti (By the Sea)*, Paul Gauguin, NGW, Chester Dale Collection; *r*: Gauguin's palette, MO/RMN

**Pages 44–45 Colour science**
**p44:** *tl*: Microphotograph from *A Sunday Afternoon on the Island of La Grande Jatte*, Georges Seurat, © AIC/Photo: I. Fielder; *r*: *Study for "Les Poseuses"*, Georges Seurat, MO, Paris; *bl*: Frontispiece of Rood's "Colours and Applications", BIF; *br*: *A Sunday Afternoon on the Island of La Grande Jatte*, Georges Seurat, © AIC, Helen Bartlett Memorial Collection **p45:** *t*, *c* (detail): *Against the Enamel of a Background Rhythmic with Beats and Angles, Tones and Colours, Portrait of Félix Fénéon in 1890*, Paul Signac, PC, New York/Photo: Malcolm Varon, NYC/© DACS 1993; *br*: Charles Henry's Aesthetic Protractor from "*Rapporteur Esthétique*", PC

**Pages 46–47 A means of expression**
**p46:** *tl*: *The Night Café*, Vincent van Gogh, Yale University Art Gallery, Bequest of Stephen Carlton Clark BA, 1903 **p46:** *l*: *The Scream*, Edvard Munch, © Munch Museum, Munch Estate, Bono, Oslo/DACS, London 1993; *tr*: *Two Women on the Shore*, Edvard Munch, NGW, Gift of the Sarah G. Epstein and Lionel C. Epstein Family Collection, in Honour of the 50th Anniversary of the NGW; *cr*: *Two Women on the Shore*, Edvard Munch, NGW, Print Purchase Fund (Rosenwald Collection) and Ailsa Mellon Bruce Fund© Munch Museum, Munch Estate, Bono, Oslo/DACS, London 1993; *b*: *Dresden Houses*,

*Continued on p. 64*

# Index

---

Ernst Ludwig Kirchner, NGW, Ruth and Jacob Kainen Collection, Gift (Partial and Promised) in Honour of the 50th Anniversary of the NGW

**Pages 48–49 Patterns of the East**
p48: *c: Sketch for the Balcony*, James Abbott McNeill Whistler, HA, Birnie Philip Bequest; *l: View over the Bay of Shinagawa, The Fourth Month*, from the series "The 12 Months of Mimami", Kiyonaga, BM; *br: Catching Fireflies*, Choki, BM p49: *tl: Fulfilment*, Gustav Klimt, Musée de Strasbourg; *tr: Atsuita Karaori kimono*, Collection of Tokyo National Museum; *c: Japanese folding screen*, Collection les Indiennes, Paris; *bl: Le Père Tanguy*, Vincent van Gogh, PC, Paris/BAL; *br: Promenade des Nourrices, Frise des Fiacres (Street Scene)*, Pierre Bonnard, MO, Paris/RMN/© ADAGP /SPADEM, Paris, and DACS, London 1993

**Pages 50–51 Picasso's changing palette**
p50: *tr:* Photo of Picasso in his studio, Photo: Michel Sima/Selon; *l: Madame Camus*, Edgar Degas, NGW, Chester Dale Collection; *br: The Tragedy*, Pablo Picasso, NGW, Chester Dale Collection/© DACS 1993 p51: *l: Nude Woman*, Pablo Picasso, NGW, Ailsa Mellon Bruce Fund/© DACS 1993; *tr: Houses in Provence*, Paul Cézanne, NGW, Collection of Mr. and Mrs. Paul Mellon; *c: Las Meninas*, Diego Velázquez, Museo del Prado, Madrid; *br: Las Meninas: Infanta Margerita Maria No. 27*, Pablo Picasso, Museu Pablo Picasso, Barcelona/© DACS 1993

**Pages 52–53 Colour and music**
p52: *tr:* Newton's colour wheel; *bl:* Frontispiece and page from "*De Colori*", by Matteo Zaccolini, Biblioteca Medicea Laurenziana, Florence; *br: Mary, Queen of Heaven*, Master of the Saint Lucy Legend, NGW, Samuel H. Kress Collection p53: *t: Junger Wald (Young Forest)*, Paul Klee, NGW, Gift (Partial and Promised) of Lili-Charlotte Sarnoff in Honour of the 50th Anniversary of the NGW/© DACS 1993 *cl: Improvisation 31 (Sea Battle)*, Wassily Kandinsky, NGW, Ailsa Mellon Bruce Fund/© ADAGP, Paris and DACS, London 1993; *c: Colour Sonatina in Red*, Ludwig Hirschfeld-Mack, Bauhaus Archiv, Museum für Gestaltung, Berlin; *bl:* Photo of Arnold Schönberg, Photographie Musée Nationale d'Art Moderne, Centre Georges Pompidou, Paris/© SPADEM, Paris, and DACS, London

1993; *br: The Song of the Vowels*, Joan Miró, Museum of Modern Art, New York, Mrs. Simon Guggenheim Fund, special contribution in Honour of Dorothy C. Miller/© ADAGP, Paris, and DACS, London 1993

**Pages 54–55 Oriental light**
p54: *tr:* Kairouan, the Grand Mosque, World Pictures; *cl:* Moucharabieh in blue and green, Musée Matisse, Nice; *c:* Photo of Klee and Macke, 1914, Bildarchiv Felix Klee, Bern, Photo: Louis Moilliet; *b: Kairouan I*, Auguste Macke, Staatsgalerie für Moderne Kunst, Munich/© Artothek p55: *t: Persische Nachtigallen (Persian Nightingales)*, Paul Klee, NGW, Gift (Partial and Promised) in Honour of the 50th Anniversary of the NGW, PC, New York/© DACS 1993; *b:* Paintbox, Winsor and Newton, Harrow, Middlesex; *br:* Persian tiling, Robert Harding Associates, London

**Pages 56–57 Matisse's pure colour**
p56: *tr: Henri Matisse*, André Derain, TG/© ADAGP, Paris, and DACS, London 1993; *l:* Baule face mask, Ivory Coast, Werner Forman Archive; *cl:* Reliquary Obi mask, Gabon, Werner Forman Archive; *br: Harmony in Red*, Henri Matisse, Hermitage, Leningrad/Artothek/© Succession H. Matisse/DACS 1993 p57: *tl:* Photo of Henri Matisse, © Hélène Adant/Rapho; *l:* Moroccan bonnet from the Collection H. Matisse, Musée Matisse, Nice; *c:* Rose and green gandoura, Morocco, Musée Matisse, Nice; *r: Beasts of the Sea*, Henri Matisse, NGW, Ailsa Mellon Bruce Fund © Succession H. Matisse/DACS 1993

**Pages 58–59 Abstract power**
p58: *tr: Wall-hanging in Red and Green*, Gunta Stölz, Bauhaus Archiv, Museum für Gestaltung, Berlin, Photo: Hermann Kiessling/© DACS 1993; *l: Diamond Painting in Red, Yellow, and Blue*, Piet Mondrian, NGW, Gift of Herbert and Nannette Rothschild/© DACS 1993; *br:* First plate of "The Interaction of Colour", Joseph Albers, Bauhaus Archiv, Museum für Gestaltung, Berlin, Photo: Markus Hawlik/© DACS 1993 p59: *t, l (detail): Red, Black, White on Yellow*, Mark Rothko, NGW, Gift of Mrs. Paul Mellon, in Honour of the 50th Anniversary of the NGW/© 1993 Kate Rothko-Prizel and Christopher Rothko/ARS New York; *bl: IKB 79*,

Yves Klein, TG/© ADAGP, Paris, and DACS, London 1993; *br: As if to Celebrate, I Discovered a Mountain Blooming with Red Flowers*, Anish Kapoor, TG

**Pages 60–61 Fresh approaches**
p60: *tl: Green Marilyn*, Andy Warhol, NGW, Gift of William C. Seitz and Irma S. Seitz in Honour of the 50th Anniversary of the NGW/© 1993 The Andy Warhol Foundation for the Visual Arts, Inc.; *br: People, Birds, and Sun*, Karel Appel, TG/De Tulp Pers, Holland pp60–61 *Summertime No. 9A*, Jackson Pollock, TG/© 1993 Pollock Krasner Foundation/ARS, New York p61: *tl: Luxor*, © Bridget Riley, 1993 Glasgow Museums: Art Gallery and Museum, Kelvingrove; *tr:* Photo of Bridget Riley, © Bridget Riley; *tc:* Tomb painting, Photo © Bridget Riley; *br: Alpha-Phi*, Morris Louis, TG

**Pages 62–63 Glossary; Featured works**
p62: *tl:* Itten's colour star (p7); *cr (detail): The Feast of the Gods* (p29); p63: *tl: Romano-Egyptian Funerary Portrait* (p9); *tr: The Rest on the Flight Into Egypt* (p24); *cr: A Sunday Afternoon on the Island of La Grande Jatte* (p44)

**Dorling Kindersley would like to thank:**
The staff at the National Gallery of Art, Washington, DC: especially Francis Smyth and Samantha Williams in the Editor's Office for their unstinting help and attention to detail; Barbara Berrie and Melanie Gifford in the Conservation Department for their meticulous technical advice; and all the other curators and conservators who helped on this project. Special thanks also to: Dr. Ashok Roy, Scientific Adviser to the National Gallery, London, for his expert technical advice, particularly with regard to pigments; Inge Fiedler at the Art Institute of Chicago; Philip Steadman for advice on camera obscuras; Bridget Riley for the loan of photographs; Inder Jamwal at John Oliver Ltd., London; Alan Fitzpatrick and Pip Seymour at A.P. Fitzpatrick Art Materials for their interest and enthusiasm, as well as the loan of a wide range of materials; the staff at Cornelissen's. Thanks are also due to: Peter Jones for his research and editorial contributions; Job Rabkin for additional picture research; Susannah Steel; the Dorling Kindersley studio for additional photography; and Hilary Bird for the index.

# Acknowledgements

**Key:** *t:* top; *b:* bottom; *c:* centre; *l:* left; *r:* right

**Photography for Dorling Kindersley:**
Philip Gatward: p6: *tr* Philippe Sebert: p9: *br;* p44: *tr* Susanna Price: p8: *bl;* p9: *cl, bcr;* p13: *t, tr;* p14: *cl;* p16: *cl;* p17: *c;* p41: *br* Edward Woodman: p11: *cr* Andy Crawford: p20: *cl;* p50: *tc* Alison Harris: p21: *br;* p44: *bl* Dave King: p52: *tl*

**Artworks:**
Simon Murrell: p45: *bc* Tony Graham: p6: *cl;* p13: *tc;* p46: *c* Claire Pegrum: p46: *tr;* p48: *tl*

**Loan of materials:**
A.P. Fitzpatrick Art Materials, Studio 1, 10–22 Barnabas Road, London E9 5SB: p8: *bl;* p9: *cl; bcr;* p13: *tl, tr;* p14: *cl;* p17: *c;* p22: *tl;* p25: *cl* Tony Street, Covent Garden Market: p8: *bl;* p17: *c* Camden Passage Antiques, London p50: *tcr* G.D. Warder and Sons, Gilders p11: *cr* L. Cornelissen & Son Ltd., 105 Great Russell Street, London WC1B 3RY: p8: *bl;* p22: *tl;* p25: *cl* Tony Street, Covent Garden Market: p8: *bl;* p17: *c*

**Author's acknowledgements:**
I would like to thank the following people for their kind help with this book: Francis Smyth, at the National Gallery of Art, Washington, DC, for her hospitality and advice; Barbara Berrie and Melanie Gifford, in the Conservation Department, and Ashok Roy and Marika Spring, in the Scientific and Conservation Departments of the National Gallery, London, for their unstinting attention to detail and generous technical comments; and Ian Chilvers for the loan of invaluable reference material.

Additional thanks are due to Keith, Jay, and Louis Shadwick for their patience and support, and to the following members of the Eyewitness Art team: Claire Pegrum (for her innovative designs), Gwen Edmonds (for overseeing the project), Julia Harris-Voss, Jo Evans, Job Rabkin, and Louise Candlish (for their painstaking research). With a special thank you to my editor, Luisa Caruso, for her thoroughness and perfectionism.

# 251 CHELSEA BUNS

**Preparation time:**
40-45 minutes, plus
1½ hours to rise
and prove

**Cooking time:**
30-35 minutes

**Oven temperature:**
190 C, 375 F, gas 5

**Makes 9**

**Calories:**
185 per bun

**YOU WILL NEED:**
2 teaspoons dried yeast
5 tablespoons warm milk
½ teaspoon sugar
225 g/8 oz strong plain flour
½ teaspoon salt
1 egg, beaten
15 g/½ oz butter, melted
golden syrup, to glaze
FOR THE FILLING
15 g/½ oz butter, melted
50 g/2 oz soft brown sugar
100 g/4 oz mixed dried fruit

Blend the yeast with the warm milk, sugar and 50 g/2 oz of the flour. Leave until frothy, about 20 minutes.

Mix the remaining flour and the salt together. Add to the yeast mixture with the beaten egg and melted butter. Mix well and knead the dough on a lightly floured board for about 10 minutes. Put to rise in a large greased polythene bag, loosely tied, until doubled in size, about 1 hour.

Knead the dough on a lightly floured surface. Roll into a rectangle about 23 × 30 cm/9 × 12 inches, brush with the melted butter and sprinkle on the sugar and fruit. Roll up as for a Swiss roll and cut into 9 slices. Place in a greased 23 cm/9 inch square cake tin. Leave to rise inside a greased polythene bag until the buns feel springy.

Remove the polythene bag and bake the buns in a moderately hot oven for 30-35 minutes. Place on a wire rack and brush the hot buns with the syrup.

---

■ COOK'S TIP

Leave yeast doughs to rise in a warm place; near a central heating boiler, radiator or in front of a fire. Alternatively warm the grill compartment of the cooker but make sure that it is not too hot or the dough will dry out on top and begin to cook instead of rise.

# 252 JAM DOUGHNUTS

**Preparation time:**
15 minutes, plus 1½
hours to rise and
prove

**Cooking time:**
10-15 minutes

**Makes 16**

**Calories:**
210 per doughnut

**YOU WILL NEED:**
450 g/1 lb strong plain flour
pinch of salt
50 g/2 oz butter or margarine
15 g/½ oz fresh yeast
50 g/2 oz caster sugar
300 ml/½ pint warm milk
2 eggs, beaten
2-3 tablespoons jam
oil for deep frying

Sift the flour and salt into a bowl, then rub in the butter or margarine. Cream the yeast with 15 g/½ oz of the sugar. Make a well in the centre of the flour, pour in the warm milk and beaten eggs. Add the yeast, mix to a light dough, cover and leave to rise in a warm place for 1 hour.

Divide the dough into 16 and shape into rounds. Place a small teaspoonful of jam in the centre of each round and draw up the edges to form a ball, pinching the dough together to seal. Put into oiled tartlet tins to prove in a warm place for 20-30 minutes.

Heat the oil to 180 C/360 F. Deep fry the doughnuts for 3-5 minutes, drain on absorbent kitchen paper and roll in the remaining caster sugar.

---

■ COOK'S TIP

To make jam and cream doughnuts, shape the unfilled dough into long doughnuts. Deep fry and roll in sugar. Split when cool and fill.

## 253 MALT BREAD

**Preparation time:**
15 minutes, plus 2
hours to rise

**Cooking time:**
35 minutes

**Oven temperature:**
200 C, 400 F, gas 6
and
180 C, 350 F, gas 4

**Makes 3 loaves**

**Calories:**
1060 per loaf

YOU WILL NEED:
*350 g/12 oz strong plain flour*
*350 g/12 oz wholemeal flour*
*¼ teaspoon salt*
*25 g/1 oz fresh yeast*
*300 ml/½ pint warm water*
*50 g/2 oz black treacle*
*100 g/4 oz malt extract*
*50 g/2 oz butter*
*100 g/4 oz sultanas*
FOR THE GLAZE
*2 teaspoons sugar*
*2 tablespoons boiling water*

Grease three 450 g/1 lb loaf tins. Sift the flours and salt into a bowl. Cream the yeast with a little of the water. Add to the flour. Gently heat the treacle, malt extract and butter until the fat has melted. Add to the flour with the remaining water and the sultanas and knead to form a very soft, sticky dough. Beat for 3 minutes. Spoon into the tins and level the top with a floured spoon. Cover with oiled cling film and leave to rise for at least 2 hours.

Bake in a moderately hot oven for 15 minutes, then reduce heat to moderate and bake for a further 20 minutes. Cover loosely with foil during cooking if becoming too brown.

Transfer to a wire rack and glaze with the sugar dissolved in the boiling water. Serve sliced and buttered.

## 254 TRADITIONAL TEABREAD

**Preparation time:**
20 minutes

**Cooking time:**
1-1¼ hours

**Oven temperature:**
180 C, 350 F, gas 4

**Makes 2 loaves**

**Calories:**
1700 per loaf

YOU WILL NEED:
*450 g/1 lb self-raising flour*
*1 teaspoon ground mixed spice*
*1 teaspoon baking powder*
*100 g/4 oz butter or margarine*
*100 g/4 oz soft brown sugar*
*225 g/8 oz mixed dried fruit*
*2 eggs, lightly beaten*
*250 ml/8 fl oz strong cold tea*

Base-line and grease two 450 g/1 lb loaf tins. Sift together the flour, mixed spice and baking powder. Rub in the butter or margarine until the mixture resembles fine breadcrumbs. Stir in the sugar and dried fruit. Make a well in the centre and gradually add the eggs and tea to form a soft dropping consistency.

Divide the mixture between the two tins and level the surface with the back of a metal spoon. Bake in a moderate oven for 1-1¼ hurs, or until a warmed skewer inserted into the centre comes out clean. Remove from the tins and allow to cool on wire racks. Serve sliced and buttered.

### ■ COOK'S TIP

*The top of the loaf can be brushed with a little warmed clear honey instead of sugar and water.*

### ■ FREEZER TIP

*To freeze the loaf sliced, interleave the slices with pieces of plastic or greaseproof paper and reshape the loaf. Pack and freeze.*

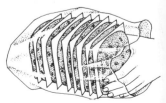

# 255 GINGERBREAD

**Preparation time:**
10 minutes

**Cooking time:**
1½ hours

**Oven temperature:**
180 C, 350 F, gas 4

**Makes 1 cake**

**Total calories:**
5465

YOU WILL NEED:
*450 g/1 lb plain flour*
*¼ teaspoon salt*
*1 tablespoon ground ginger*
*1 teaspoon ground cinnamon*
*1 teaspoon ground mixed spice*
*1 teaspoon ground cloves*
*1 tablespoon baking powder*
*1 teaspoon bicarbonate of soda*
*100 g/4 oz walnut halves, coarsely choped*
*175 g/6 oz butter*
*175 g/6 oz molasses or black treacle*
*175 g/6 oz golden syrup*
*200 g/7oz soft dark brown sugar*
*1 large egg, beaten*
*300 ml/½ pint milk*

Line and grease a 23 cm/9 inch square cake tin. Sift the flour, salt, spices, baking powder and bicarbonate of soda into a bowl. Stir in the walnuts and make a well in the centre. Heat the butter with the molasses or treacle, syrup and sugar, stirring until smooth. Add to the flour mixture with the egg and milk. Mix thoroughly.

Pour into the prepared cake tin. Bake in a moderate oven for 1½ hours, until a warmed skewer inserted in the centre comes out clean. Cool on a wire rack. Store in an airtight container until required.

# 256 PARKIN

**Preparation time:**
10 minutes

**Cooking time:**
1-1½ hours

**Oven temperature:**
180 C, 350 F, gas 4

**Makes 1 cake**

**Total calories:**
3505

YOU WILL NEED:
*175 g/6 oz plain flour*
*pinch of salt*
*1 teaspoon ground ginger*
*2 teaspoons ground cinnamon*
*1 teaspoon bicarbonate of soda*
*275 g/10 oz medium oatmeal*
*175 g/6 oz black treacle*
*100 g/4 oz butter*
*100 g/4 oz soft brown sugar*
*150 ml/¼ pint milk*
*1 egg*

Line and grease a 23 cm/9 inch square cake tin. Sift together the flour, salt, spices and soda. Add the oatmeal and toss lightly to mix. Warm together the treacle, butter, sugar and milk until the butter has melted. Cool slightly, add the egg and beat well. Pour into the centre of the dry ingredients and stir rapidly until smooth.

Pour into the prepared tin and bake in a moderate oven for 1-1½ hours, until a skewer inserted in the centre comes out clean. Cool on a wire rack.

## COOK'S TIP

*To spoon syrup, treacle or honey out of a tin or jar, first warm a metal spoon. The syrup will slide easily off the hot spoon.*

## COOK'S TIP

*Make an interesting apple and raisin parkin by mixing 50 g/2 oz raisins and 50 g/2 oz dried apple flakes into the dry ingredients. Combine as above.*

## 257 PLAIN SCONES

**Preparation time:**
15 minutes

**Cooking time:**
10-12 minutes

**Oven temperature:**
220 C, 425 F, gas 7

**Makes 8**

**Calories:**
170 per scone

YOU WILL NEED:
*225 g/8 oz plain flour*
*3 teaspoons baking powder*
*pinch of salt*
*50 g/2 oz butter or margarine*
*25 g/1 oz caster sugar*
*scant 150 ml/¼ pint milk plus milk, to*
   *glaze*

Sif the flour, baking powder and salt in a bowl. Rub in the butter or margarine until the mixture resembles fine bread-crumbs, then stir in the sugar. Mix in enough milk to make a soft dough. Turn on to a floured surface and knead very lightly.

Roll out the dough to about 1 cm/½ inch thick and cut out 8 rounds using a 6 cm/2½ inch cutter, re-rolling the dough as necessary. Place on a greased baking tray and brush with milk. Bake in a hot oven for 10-12 minutes or until well risen and golden brown. Cool on a wire rack. Serve with butter or whipped cream and jam.

## 258 CHEESE SCONES

**Preparation time:**
15 minutes

**Cooking time:**
12-15 minutes

**Oven temperature:**
220 C, 425 F, gas 7

**Makes 8**

**Calories:**
190 per scone

YOU WILL NEED:
*225 g/8 oz plain flour*
*3 teaspoons baking powder*
*pinch of salt*
*½ teaspoon mustard powder*
*40 g/1½ oz butter or margarine*
*1 onion, finely chopped*
*75 g/3 oz mature Cheddar cheese,*
   *grated*
*scant 150 ml/¼ pint milk*
*beaten egg or milk, to glaze*

Sift the flour, baking powder, salt and mustard into a bowl. Rub in the butter or margarine until the mixture resembles fine breadcrumbs. Stir in the onion and Cheddar, then mix in enough milk to make a soft dough. Roll out on a lightly floured surface to about 1 cm/½ inch thick. Cut out 8 rounds using a 6 cm/2½ inch cutter, re-rolling the dough as necessary. Place on a greased baking tray and brush with a little egg or milk. Bake in a hot oven for 12-15 minutes or until well risen and golden. Cool on a wire rack.

■ COOK'S TIP

*To make fruit scones, stir 50 g/2 oz sultanas into the rubbed-in mixture. Combine as above.*

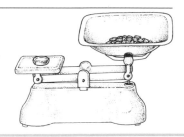

■ FREEZER TIP

*Remove the scones from the oven when two-thirds cooked, cool and freeze. Arrange frozen scones on a casserole and cook 15-20 minutes.*

# 259 DROP SCONES

**Preparation time:**
5 minutes

**Cooking time:**
5-10 minutes

**Makes about 30**

**Calories:**
40 per scone

YOU WILL NEED:
*225 g/8 oz plain flour*
*¼ teaspoon salt*
*½ teaspoon bicarbonate of soda*
*1 teaspoon cream of tartar*
*25 g/1 oz caster sugar*
*1 egg*
*300 ml/½ pint milk*

Sift together the flour, salt, bicarbonate of soda and cream of tartar. Stir in the sugar and make a well in the centre. Gradually beat in the egg and milk to make a smooth thick batter.

Lightly grease a hot griddle or heavy-based frying pan and drop large spoonsful of the mixture on, allowing plenty of room for spreading. When the surface bubbles and the drop scones are set, turn quickly and cook the other side. Serve wrapped in a clean cloth to keep scones warm and soft.

# 260 WHOLEMEAL APPLE ROUND

**Preparation time:**
15 minutes

**Cooking time:**
20-25 minutes

**Oven temperature:**
200 C, 400 F, gas 6

**Serves 8**

**Calories:**
190 per portion

YOU WILL NEED:
*1 medium cooking apple*
*225 g/8 oz wholemeal flour*
*½ teaspoon salt*
*3 teaspoons baking powder*
*50 g/2 oz butter or margarine*
*50 g/2 oz soft brown sugar*
*about 150 ml/¼ pint milk*
*FOR THE GLAZE*
*a little milk*
*1 tablespoon demerara sugar*

Peel, core and finely chop the apple. Put the flour, salt and baking powder into a bowl. Rub in the butter or margarine, then stir in the sugar and chopped apple. Add the milk and mix to form a soft but not sticky dough.

Roll out on a floured surface to a 5 mm/¼ inch thick round. Place on a greased baking tray and mark into eight wedges. Brush the top with milk and sprinkle with demerara sugar. Bake in a moderately hot oven for 20-25 minutes. Serve warm with butter.

---

■ COOK'S TIP

*To make savoury drop scones, omit the sugar, add 4 tablespoons grated Parmesan cheese and 1 teaspoon mixed dried herbs to the batter. Serve hot.*

■ COOK'S TIP

*If you are in a hurry, then prepare the scone dough and flatten it with your hand straight on the greased baking tray to save rolling it out.*

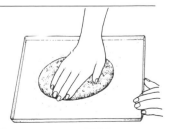

# Family Cakes & Biscuits

Making cakes and biscuits at home is double rewarding. Not only do they taste much better than the commercial variety, they are more economical too.

## 261 CARROT CAKE

**Preparation time:**
20 minutes

**Cooking time:**
1½ hours

**Oven temperature:**
160 C, 325 F, gas 3

**Makes 1 cake**

**Total calories:**
4920

YOU WILL NEED:
*225 g/8 oz butter or margarine*
*225 g/8 oz soft brown sugar*
*4 eggs, lightly beaten*
*225 g/8 oz self-raising flour, sifted*
*½ teaspoon salt*
*1 teaspoon grated nutmeg*
*3 teaspoons mixed spice*
*350 g/12 oz carrots, coarsely grated*
FOR THE GLACÉ ICING
*225 g/8 oz icing sugar*
*2 tablespoons water*
*50 g/2 oz walnut halves, to decorate*

Line and grease a deep 20 cm/8 inch round cake tin. Cream the butter or margarine and sugar until light and fluffy. Gradually beat in the eggs, adding a little of the flour to prevent curdling. Fold in the remaining flour, salt and spices. Fold in the grated carrot and spoon into the prepared cake tin. Level the top and bake in a moderate oven for 1½ hours or until a skewer inserted in the centre comes out clean. Cool in the tin for 5 minutes before turning out on to a wire rack to cool completely.

Beat the icing ingredients together until smooth, pour over the cake and decorate with walnuts, chopping some to form a decorative border.

## 262 VICTORIA SANDWICH CAKE

**Preparation time:**
15 minutes

**Cooking time:**
20-25 minutes

**Oven temperature:**
180 C, 350 F, gas 4

**Makes 1 cake**

**Total calories:**
1910

YOU WILL NEED:
*100 g/4 oz butter or margarine*
*100 g/4 oz caster sugar*
*2 eggs, lightly beaten*
*100 g/4 oz self-raising flour, sifted*
*4 tablespoons strawberry jam*
*sifted icing sugar, for dusting*

Grease and flour two 18 cm/7 inch sandwich tins. Cream the butter or margarine and sugar until light and fluffy. Gradually beat in the eggs, adding a little of the flour to prevent curdling. Carefully fold in the remaining flour using a metal spoon. Divide the mixture between the two tins and level the tops. Bake in a moderate oven for 20-25 minutes or until the cakes are risen, springy, firm to the touch and golden. Turn out and cool on a wire rack.

When cold, sandwich the two cakes together with the jam and dust with icing sugar.

### ■ COOK'S TIP

*Use a food processor, fitted with a coarse grating disc, to prepare the carrots. Halve any large ones to fit into the feed tube and pack the tube neatly.*

### ■ COOK'S TIP

*To flour cake tins, put a spoonful of flour in the greased tin. Tilt from side to side, tapping the edge to coat the tin evenly. Tip excess flour into the second tin.*

# 263 DUNDEE CAKE

**Preparation time:**
15 minutes

**Cooking time:**
3½ hours

**Oven temperature:**
150 C, 300 F, gas 2

**Makes 1 cake**

**Total calories:**
5385

YOU WILL NEED:
*225 g/8 oz butter or margarine*
*225 g/8 oz caster sugar*
*5 eggs, lightly beaten*
*350 g/12 oz self-raising flour, sifted*
*675 g/1½ lb mixed dried fruit*
*100 g/4 oz glacé cherries, washed and*
  *quartered*
*1 teaspoon mixed spice*
*50 g/2 oz whole blanched almonds*

Line and grease a deep 20 cm/8 inch round cake tin. Cream the butter or margarine with the sugar until light and fluffy. Gradually beat in the eggs, adding a little flour if necessary to prevent the mixture from curdling. Mix the dried fruit and glacé cherries with a spoonful of the flour. Fold the remaining flour and the mixed spice into the creamed mixture. Stir in the dried fruit and glacé cherries. Spoon the mixture into the prepared tin and level the surface. Top with concentric circles of almonds.

Bake in a cool oven for 3½ hours or until a skewer inserted into the centre of the cake comes out clean. Leave to cool in the tin for about 10 minutes, then turn out on to a wire rack to cool completely.

# 264 QUICK FRUIT CAKE

**Preparation time:**
15 minutes

**Cooking time:**
1-1¼ hours

**Oven temperature:**
180 C, 350 F, gas 4

**Makes 1 cake**

**Total calories:**
2410

YOU WILL NEED:
*100 g/4 oz butter or margarine*
*100 g/4 oz caster sugar*
*2 eggs, lightly beaten*
*225 g/8 oz self-raising flour, sifted*
*100 g/4 oz mixed dried fruit*
*50 g/2 oz glacé cherries, washed and*
  *sliced*

Line and grease a deep 18 cm/7 inch round cake tin. Cream the butter or margarine with the sugar until light and fluffy. Gradually beat in the eggs, adding a little of the flour to prevent curdling. Mix the dried fruit and cherries wth a spoonful of the flour. Fold the remaining flour into the creamed mixture, then fold in the fruit. Spoon the mixture into the prepared tin.

Level the top of the cake and bake in a moderate oven for 1-1¼ hours or until a skewer inserted into the centre of the cake comes out clean. Leave to cool in the tin for 5 minutes, then turn out and cool completely on a wire rack.

---

■ COOK'S TIP

*If you have whole almonds with peel on, cover them with boiling water and leave for 1 minute. Drain and rub off the skins between thumbs and forefinger.*

---

■ COOK'S TIP

*To level the surface of a fruit cake mixture, dampen a large metal spoon in hot water, shake off the water and use the rounded side to level the mixture.*

## 265 CHOCOLATE CAKE

| Preparation time: | YOU WILL NEED: |
|---|---|
| 30 minutes | 100 g/4 oz butter or margarine |
| | 100 g/4 oz caster sugar |
| **Cooking time:** | 2 eggs, lightly beaten |
| 25-30 minutes | 100 g/4 oz self-raising flour, sifted |
| **Oven temperature:** | 50 g/2 oz cocoa powder, sifted |
| 160 C, 325 F, gas 3 | 2 tablespoons boiling water |
| | 100 g/4 oz butter |
| **Makes 1** | 450 g/1 lb icing sugar, sifted |
| **Total calories:** | 50 g/2 oz plain chocolate, grated |
| 4180 | 2-3 tablespoons water |
| | brown food colouring |

Base-line and grease two 18 cm/7 inch sandwich tins. Cream the butter or margarine with the sugar until light and fluffy. Gradually beat in the eggs. Fold in the flour and 25 g/1 oz cocoa. Divide the mixture between the tins. Bake in a moderate oven for 25-30 minutes. Cool on a wire rack.

Mix the remaining cocoa powder and boiling water together. Beat the butter and 225 g/8 oz icing sugar until pale, beat in the cocoa. Use one-third of the buttercream to sandwich the cakes together. Spread another third over the side of the cake. Press the grated chocolate on the side. Mix the remaining icing sugar and water. Colour a few teaspoons brown and place in a piping bag fitted with a small plain nozzle. Spread the rest over the cake and pipe on parallel rows of brown. Draw the point of a skewer across the rows to give a feathered effect. Pipe a border with the remaining buttercream.

## 266 COFFEE AND ALMOND CAKE

| Preparation time: | YOU WILL NEED: |
|---|---|
| 25 minutes | 100 g/4 oz butter or margarine |
| | 100 g/4 oz caster sugar |
| **Cooking time:** | 2 eggs, lightly beaten |
| 30 minutes | 100 g/4 oz self-raising flour |
| | ½ teaspoon baking powder |
| **Oven temperature:** | 50 g/2 oz ground almonds |
| 160 C, 325 F, gas 3 | 1 tablespoon instant coffee, dissolved |
| | in 1 tablespoon hot water |
| **Makes 1 cake** | FOR THE FILLING AND DECORATION |
| **Total calories:** | 100 g/4 oz butter |
| 3845 | 225 g/8 oz icing sugar, sifted |
| | 1 tablespoon instant coffee, dissolved |
| | in 1 tablespoon hot water |
| | 50 g/2 oz flaked almonds |

Base-line and grease two 18 cm/7 inch sandwich tins. Cream the fat and sugar until light and fluffy. Gradually beat in the eggs. Fold in the flour, baking powder, ground almonds and coffee. Divide the mixture between the tins. Bake in a moderate oven for 30 minutes or until well risen and firm to the touch. Cool on a wire rack.

Cream the butter and icing sugar until light and fluffy. Stir in the coffee. Use one-third of the mixture to sandwich the cakes together. Use the remainder to spread over the top and sides of the cake and to pipe a border on top of the cake. Press the flaked almonds on the side of the cake.

■ COOK'S TIP

*Fold a 20 cm/8 inch paper square in half. Fold corners of long side as shown and crease fold lines. Unfold, form into a cone and secure. Snip off corner to take a nozzle.*

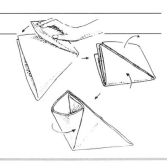

■ COOK'S TIP

*To level out a creamed cake mixture in sandwich tins, tap the base of the tin firmly on the edge of a table or work surface. The mixture will level in the tin.*

## 267 NUTTY MARMALADE CAKE

**Preparation time:**
20 minutes

**Cooking time:**
1½ hours

**Oven temperature:**
160 C, 325 F, gas 3

**Makes 1 cake**

**Total calories:**
5275

YOU WILL NEED:
225 g/8 oz butter or margarine
3 tablespoons thick-cut marmalade
225 g/8 oz demerara sugar
4 eggs, lightly beaten
225 g/8 oz self-raising flour, sifted
2 teaspoons ground cinnamon
a little grated nutmeg
100 g/4 oz chopped walnuts
FOR THE GLACÉ ICING
225 g/8 oz icing sugar, sifted
1 tablespoon lemon juice
1 tablespoon orange juice
grated orange rind, to decorate

Line and grease a 20 cm/8 inch square cake tin. Cream the butter or margarine, marmalade and sugar until light and fluffy. Gradually beat in the eggs, adding a little of the flour to prevent curdling. Fold in the remaining flour, the cinnamon and nutmeg, then fold in the walnuts.

Spoon into the prepared tin, level the top and bake in a moderate oven for 1½ hours or until a skewer inserted into the centre comes out clean. Cool in the tin for 5 minutes before turning out on to a wire rack to cool completely. Beat the ingredients for the glacé icing together until smooth. Pour the icing over the top of the cake and allow to drizzle down the sides. Decorate with orange rind.

## 268 BANANA AND WALNUT CAKE

**Preparation time:**
20 minutes

**Cooking time:**
1¼-1½ hours

**Oven temperature:**
180 C, 350 F, gas 4

**Makes 1 cake**

**Total calories:**
2720

YOU WILL NEED:
100 g/4 oz butter or margarine
100 g/4 oz light soft brown sugar
2 eggs, lightly beaten
225 g/8 oz plain wholemeal flour
1½ teaspoons baking powder
1 teaspoon grated nutmeg
2 bananas, peeled and chopped
100 g/4 oz chopped walnuts
soft brown sugar, to decorate

Line and grease a deep 18 cm/7 inch round cake tin. Cream the butter or margarine and sugar until light and fluffy. Gradually beat in the eggs. Fold in the flour, baking powder and nutmeg. Carefully fold in the bananas and walnuts.

Spoon into the prepared tin, level the top and bake in a moderate oven for 1¼-1½ hours or until a skewer inserted into the centre comes out clean. Turn out on to a wire rack, sprinkle the top with soft brown sugar and leave to cool.

### ◼ COOK'S TIP

Long strands of orange rind are a useful decoration. Pare the rind thinly, cut into strips and cook in boiling water for 3-5 minutes. Drain and cool.

### ◼ COOK'S TIP

Freshly grated nutmeg gives a superior flavour to that which is bought ready grated. Miniature graters especially for nutmegs are available.

## 269 MADEIRA CAKE

**Preparation time:**
15 minutes

**Cooking time:**
1½ hours

**Oven temperature:**
160 C, 325 F, gas 3

**Makes 1 cake**

**Total calories:**
3045

**YOU WILL NEED:**
*175 g/6 oz butter*
*175 g/6 oz caster sugar*
*3 eggs, lightly beaten*
*225 g/8 oz self-raising flour, sifted*
*about 3 tablespoons milk*
*pieces of candied peel*

Line and grease a deep 15 cm/6 inch round cake tin. Cream the butter and sugar until light and fluffy. Gradually beat in the eggs, adding a little of the remaining flour and add enough milk to make a soft dropping consistency. Spoon the mixture into the prepared tin and lay the candied peel on top.

Bake in a moderate oven for 1¼-1½ hours or until the cake is firm to touch and a skewer inserted into the centre comes out clean. Leave the cake to cool in the tin for about 5 minutes before transferring to a wire rack to cool completely.

## 270 DATE AND WALNUT LOAF

**Preparation time:**
15 minutes

**Cooking time:**
about 1 hour

**Oven temperature:**
180 C, 350 F, gas 4

**Makes 1 loaf**

**Total calories:**
2875

**YOU WILL NEED:**
*100 g/4 oz butter or margarine*
*100 g/4 oz caster sugar*
*2 eggs, lightly beaten*
*225 g/8 oz self-raising flour, sifted*
*1 teaspoon mixed spice*
*100 g/4 oz walnuts, roughly chopped*
*100 g/4 oz dates, roughly chopped*
*about 3 tablespoons milk*

Line and grease a 1 kg/2 lb loaf tin. Cream the butter or margarine and sugar until pale and fluffy. Gradually beat in the eggs. Fold in the flour, spice, walnuts and dates. Add a little milk to make a dropping consistency.

Bake in a moderate oven for about 1 hour. Insert a skewer in the centre of the cake; if it comes out clean the loaf is cooked. Cool slightly before turning out on to a wire rack to cool completely.

■ COOK'S TIP

*Halve 225 g/8 oz glacé cherries and wash under warm water. Dry thoroughly, toss with a little of the flour, then fold in last. Bake as above. Omit peel.*

■ COOK'S TIP

*Stand tin on greaseproof paper big enough to come up 2.5cm/1 inch above edges of tin. Draw round base; cut in from corners. Line greased tin, overlapping cut corners.*

## 271 SWISS ROLL

**Preparation time:**
10 minutes

**Cooking time:**
7-10 minutes

**Oven temperature:**
220 C, 425 F, gas 7

**Makes 1**

**Total calories:**
1090

YOU WILL NEED:
*3 eggs*
*75 g/3 oz caster sugar*
*75 g/3 oz plain flour, sifted*
*4 tablespoons raspberry jam*
*caster sugar for dredging*

Line and grease a 23 × 30 cm/9 × 12 inch Swiss roll tin. Whisk the eggs and sugar until very pale and thick enough to leave a trail when the whisk is lifted out. Carefully fold in the flour using a metal spoon. Turn the mixture into the prepared tin, spreading it out very lightly. Bake in a hot oven for 7-10 minutes.

Meanwhile place a clean tea-towel on a work surface, cover with greaseproof paper and dredge with sugar. Turn the hot Swiss roll on to the paper. Trim off the edges, spread with jam and, using the cloth and paper as a guide, quickly roll up tightly. Dredge with caster sugar and cool on a wire rack.

## 272 ROCK CAKES

**Preparation time:**
15 minutes

**Cooking time:**
20 minutes

**Oven temperature:**
190 C, 375 F, gas 5

**Makes 8**

**Calories:**
330 per cake

YOU WILL NEED:
*225 g/8 oz self-raising flour*
*1 teaspoon mixed spice*
*½ teaspoon grated nutmeg*
*150 g/5 oz margarine*
*75 g/3 oz demerara sugar*
*150 g/5 oz mixed dried fruit*
*1 egg, lightly beaten*
*2 tablespoons milk*

Grease two baking trays. Sift the flour and spices into a bowl. Rub in the margarine until the mixture resembles fine breadcrumbs. Stir in the sugar and fruit, then mix in the egg and milk to make a fairly stiff mixture. Place eight spoonsful of the mixture well apart on the baking tray and bake in a moderately hot oven for 20 minutes. Cool on a wire rack. These cakes are best eaten on the same day as baking.

■ COOK'S TIP

*Draw round base of tin on a sheet of greaseproof paper, snip in from corners. Place in greased tin, overlapping corners, then grease. The paper should be 5 cm/2 inches higher than tin.*

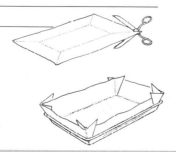

■ COOK'S TIP

*When rubbing fat into flour use only fingertips. Keep fingers spaced apart and lift the ingredients, rubbing quickly and lightly to make a light unsticky mixture.*

## 273 FRUIT BUNS

**Preparation time:**
15 minutes

**Cooking time:**
15-20 minutes

**Oven temperature:**
190 C, 375 F, gas 5

**Makes 18**

**Calories:**
100 per bun

**YOU WILL NEED:**
*100 g/4 oz butter or margarine*
*100 g/4 oz caster sugar*
*2 eggs, lightly beaten*
*100 g/4 oz self-raising flour*
*75 g/3 oz currants*

Place 18 paper cake cases on a baking tray or in two deep bun tin trays.

Cream the butter or margarine with the sugar until light and fluffy. Gradually beat in the eggs. Carefully fold in the flour and currants, using a metal spoon. Divide the mixture between the paper cases.

Bake in a moderately hot oven for 15-20 minutes or until well risen and golden brown. Transfer to a wire rack to cool.

## 274 BAKEWELL TARTS

**Preparation time:**
15 minutes

**Cooking time:**
30 minutes

**Oven temperature:**
190 C, 375 F, gas 5

**Makes 18**

**Calories:**
155 per tart

**YOU WILL NEED:**
*FOR THE SHORTCRUST PASTRY*
*225 g/8 oz plain flour*
*pinch of salt*
*100 g/4 oz margarine*
*2-3 tablespoons cold water*
*FOR THE FILLING*
*4 tablespoons strawberry jam*
*50 g/2 oz butter or margarine*
*50 g/2 oz caster sugar*
*1 egg, lightly beaten*
*25 g/1 oz ground almonds*
*50 g/2 oz self-raising flour, sifted*
*few drops of almond essence*
*1 tablespoon milk*

Sift the flour and salt into a bowl. Cut the margarine into small pieces and rub into the flour until the mixture resembles fine breadcrumbs. Add enough water to mix to a soft dough.

Roll out and use to line 18 patty tins. Put half a teaspoon of jam into each pastry case. Beat the butter or margarine with the sugar until pale and creamy. Gradually beat in the egg. Fold in the almonds, flour, almond essence and milk.

Place a small spoonful of this mixture on top of the jam and smooth it to the edge of the pastry. Bake in a moderate oven for 25-30 minutes or until well-risen and golden. Cool on a wire rack.

---

■ COOK'S TIP

*Cream fat and sugar at room temperature and soft. Use the flat side of a wooden spoon and beat in one direction; keep the mixture down in the base of the bowl.*

■ COOK'S TIP

*To fold in dry ingredients use a metal spoon. Sprinkle some lightly over the surface, then cut and fold in a figure of eight, adding the remaining ingredients.*

# 275 JAM TARTS

**Preparation time:**
15 minutes

**Cooking time:**
15 minutes

**Oven temperature:**
200 C, 400 F, gas 6

**Makes 24**

**Calories:**
40 per tart

**YOU WILL NEED:**
*100 g/4 oz plain flour*
*pinch of salt*
*50 g/2 oz butter or margarine*
*1-2 tablespoons water*
*100 g/4 oz strawberry jam*

Sift the flour and salt into a bowl. Rub in the butter or margarine until the mixture resembles fine breadcrumbs. Stir in just enough water to bind the ingredients, and lightly mix together. Roll out the pastry on a lightly floured surface, then cut out 24 6 cm/2½ inch rounds. Use these to line patty tins. Put a small spoonful of jam into each tart. Bake in a moderate oven for 10-15 minutes or until the pastry is golden. Cool on a wire rack. Serve warm or cold.

# 276 LAMINGTONS

**Preparation time:**
25 minutes

**Cooking time:**
45 minutes

**Oven temperature:**
180 C, 350 F, gas 4

**Makes 18**

**Calories:**
290 per cake

**YOU WILL NEED:**
*175 g/6 oz butter or margarine*
*225 g/8 oz caster sugar*
*1 teaspoon vanilla essence*
*3 eggs, beaten*
*350 g/12 oz plain flour*
*2 teaspoons baking powder*
*¼ teaspoon salt*
*150 ml/¼ pint milk*
*225 g/8 oz icing sugar*
*25 g/1 oz cocoa powder*
*about 150 ml/¼ pint cold water*
*100 g/4 oz dessicated coconut*

Cream the fat in a bowl and gradually add the sugar. Beat until light and fluffy, then beat in the vanilla essence. Gradually beat the eggs into the creamed mixture until smooth. Sift together the flour, baking powder and salt and add to the mixture, a third at a time, alternating with milk. Beat well after each addition. Pour into a greased 28 × 18 cm/11 × 7 inch tin and bake in a moderate oven for 45 minutes.

Invert the tin on to a wire rack to cool and leave for 5-10 minutes before removing the tin.

When completely cool, cut the cake into three strips lengthways, then cut each strip into six pieces. Sift the icing sugar and cocoa into a bowl, pour in the water. Stir over a pan of hot water until the icing is smooth and shiny. Scatter the coconut thickly on a large piece of greaseproof paper. Using a fork, dip each cube of cake into the icing. Allow a moment for the icing to set slightly, then roll each cube in the coconut. Dry on a wire rack.

■ COOK'S TIP

*Use only enough water to bind pastry. Handle dough lightly. Use a very light sifting of flour for rolling and roll one way only. Do not turn pastry over.*

■ COOK'S TIP

*When coating cakes in dry ingredients, tilt the greaseproof paper from hand to hand to rock the piece of cake in the coating ingredient and coat evenly.*

## 277 VIENNESE WHIRLS

**Preparation time:**
15 minutes, plus
15-20 minutes to
chill

**Cooking time:**
12-15 minutes

**Oven temperature:**
190 C, 375 F, gas 5

**Makes 18-20**

**Total calories:**
2040

YOU WILL NEED:
*100 g/4 oz butter or margarine*
*50 g/2 oz icing sugar, sifted*
*100 g/4 oz plain flour, sifted*
*½ teaspoon vanilla essence*
FOR THE FILLING
*50 g/2 oz butter or margarine*
*25 g/1 oz icing sugar, sifted*
*50 g/2 oz chocolate, melted*
*icing sugar, to dust*

Grease two baking trays. Beat the butter or margarine with the sugar until pale and very soft. Stir in the flour and vanilla essence. Spoon the mixture into a piping bag fitted with a large star nozzle and pipe 18-20 rings on to the baking trays. Chill for 15-20 minutes. Bake in a moderately hot oven for 12-15 minutes. Leave the biscuits on the tray, for a few seconds, then use a palette knife to lift them off. Cool on a wire rack.

For the filling, beat the butter or margarine with the icing sugar. Cool the melted chocolate slightly, then stir into the filling. Pipe a little on half the whirls, top with the remaining halves. Dust with icing sugar.

## 278 SHORTBREAD

**Preparation time:**
15 minutes, plus 15
minutes to chill

**Cooking time:**
40 minutes

**Oven temperature:**
160 C, 325 F, gas 3

**Makes 8 pieces**

**Calories:**
195 per piece

YOU WILL NEED:
*175 g/6 oz plain flour, sifted*
*pinch of salt*
*100 g/4 oz butter*
*50 g/2 oz caster sugar*
*grated rind of 1 lemon*
*icing sugar, to dust*

Grease and flour a baking tray. Put the flour and salt in a mixing bowl. Rub in the butter, then stir in the sugar and lemon rind. Lightly work the mixture together until it forms a smooth stiff ball of dough. Roll into a 20 cm/8 inch circle and place on the baking tray. Pinch the edges, prick the middle all over with a fork and cut the shortbread into eight wedges. Chill for 15 minutes.

Bake in a moderate oven for 40 minutes or until pale golden. Leave on the baking tray for a few minutes, then cool completely on a wire rack.

■ COOK'S TIP

*To pipe biscuits, hold the bag at right angles to the tray. Squeeze the bag evenly and firmly, lift off sharply or slide a knife across the nozzle to finish.*

■ COOK'S TIP

*Prick biscuits evenly and decoratively with a fork before cooking to prevent them bubbling up or rising when baked. Chilling first makes a crisp, short biscuit.*

## 279 GINGERBREAD MEN

**Preparation time:**
15 minutes

**Cooking time:**
10 minutes

**Oven temperature:**
190 C, 375 F, gas 5

**Makes 14**

**Calories:**
150 per gingerbread
man

**YOU WILL NEED:**
100 g/4 oz butter or margarine
100 g/4 oz dark soft brown sugar
2 tablespoons golden syrup
225 g/8 oz plain flour, sifted
2 teaspoons ground ginger
currants or raisins, to decorate

Grease two baking trays. Cream the butter or margarine with the sugar until light and fluffy. Beat in the syrup. Stir in the flour and ginger. Lightly knead the mixture on a floured surface then roll out to 5 mm/¼ inch thick.

Cut out 14 gingerbread men (use gingerbread women cutters too, if you like). Add raisins or currants to represent buttons, eyes, nose and mouth. Transfer to the baking trays and bake in a moderate oven for 10 minutes or until firm and golden. Cool on a wire rack.

## 280 BOURBONS

**Preparation time:**
20 minutes, plus 1
hour to chill

**Cooking time:**
10-15 minutes

**Oven temperature:**
180 C, 350 F, gas 4

**Makes 16**

**Calories:**
200 per biscuit

**YOU WILL NEED:**
175 g/6 oz plain flour
25 g/1 oz cocoa powder
75 g/3 oz butter or margarine
50 g/2 oz caster sugar
2 tablespoons golden syrup
1 egg, lightly beaten
granulated sugar for sprinkling
FOR THE FILLING
100 g/4 oz butter
175 g/6 oz icing sugar, sifted
25 g/1 oz cocoa powder
2 tablespoons boiling water

Lightly grease two baking trays. Sift the flour and cocoa powder into a bowl. Rub in the fat, then stir in the sugar, syrup and enough beaten egg to make a firm dough. Roll out on a floured work surface to a rectangle 30 × 40 cm/12 × 16 inches. Cut in half lengthways, then cut each half into 16 evenly sized fingers. Prick all over with a fork. Carefully transfer to the baking trays and chill.

Bake in a moderate oven for 10-15 minutes. Sprinkle the biscuits with the sugar. Leave on the baking trays for 1 minute. Cool completely on a wire rack.

For the filling, cream the butter and icing sugar until pale. Dissolve the cocoa in the water, cool, then beat into the filling. Use to sandwich the biscuits in pairs.

### COOK'S TIP

Keep a small lidded jam jar of vegetable oil ready for greasing tins. Alternatively, gadgets known as 'oil wells' have a brush which fits in a neat oil container.

### FREEZER TIP

To chill foods quickly, place them in the freezer for a few minutes. Do not put unopened cans in the freezer for more than a few minutes.

## 281 CHOCOLATE CASTLES

**Preparation time:**
20 minutes

**Cooking time:**
10-12 minutes

**Oven temperature:**
220 C, 425 F, gas 7

**Makes 18**

**Calories:**
145 per cake

YOU WILL NEED:
*100 g/4 oz butter or margarine*
*100 g/4 oz caster sugar*
*2 eggs, lightly beaten*
*75 g/3 oz self-raising flour, sifted*
*25 g/1 oz cocoa powder, sifted*
*about 6 tablespoons chocolate spread*
*100 g/4 oz chocolate vermiceilli*
*18 chocolate buttons*

Thoroughly grease 18 dariole tins and stand them on a baking tray. Cream the butter or margarine and sugar until light and fluffy. Gradually beat in the eggs. Fold in the flour and cocoa powder using a metal spoon.

Divide the mixture between the tins. Bake in a hot oven for 10-12 minutes. Turn out on to a wire rack and leave to cool.

Smooth the chocolate spread over the top and sides of the castles and roll in the vermicelli. Top with chocolate buttons.

## 282 SESAME FLAPJACKS

**Preparation time:**
10 minutes

**Cooking time:**
45 minutes

**Oven temperature:**
180 C, 350 F, gas 4

**Makes 12**

**Calories:**
205 per flapjack

YOU WILL NEED:
*100 g/4 oz butter or margarine*
*50 g/2 oz demerara sugar*
*4 tablespoons golden syrup*
*175 g/6 oz rolled oats*
*50 g/2 oz sesame seeds*
*100 g/4 oz dates, chopped*

Base-line and grease a 28 × 18 cm/11 × 7 inch Swiss roll tin. Melt the butter or margarine and sugar in a large saucepan over a low heat, then stir in the remaining ingredients. The mixture should be fairly stiff.

Spread the mixture in the prepared tin and bake in a moderate oven for 40 minutes. Cut into 12 equal portions while still hot, and leave to cool in the tin.

### ■ MICROWAVE TIP

*If the chocolate spread is slightly too thick to spread over the cakes, then warm it in a basin in the microwave. Allow 30 seconds on full power.*

### ■ COOK'S TIP

*Muesli flapjacks are delicious and easy. Omit sesame seeds and dates and substitute oats with muesli.*

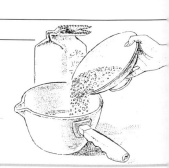

## 283 CHOCOLATE NUT CRISPIES

**Preparation time:**
10 minutes

**Cooking time:**
5 minutes

**Makes 18**

**Calories:**
60 per cake

**YOU WILL NEED:**
50 g/2 oz butter or margarine
50 g/2 oz cocoa powder
2 tablespoons golden syrup
50 g/2 oz cornflakes
50 g/2 oz walnuts, roughly chopped

Place 18 paper cases on a wire rack. Over a low heat, melt together the butter or margarine, cocoa powder and syrup. Stir in the cornflakes and walnuts, and stir until thoroughly mixed. Spoon into the paper cases and leave to set. These are best eaten the same day as making.

## 284 PEANUT COOKIES

**Preparation time:**
10 minutes

**Cooking time:**
20-25 minutes

**Oven temperature:**
180 C, 350 F, gas 4

**Makes 40**

**Calories:**
75 per cookie

**YOU WILL NEED:**
100 g/4 oz crunchy peanut butter
100 g/4 oz butter or margarine
100 g/4 oz caster sugar
75 g/3 oz soft light brown sugar
2 eggs, lightly beaten
225 g/8 oz self-raising flour, sifted
40 salted peanuts

Lightly grease two baking trays. Cream the peanut butter, butter or margarine and sugars until very soft, light and fluffy. Gradually beat in the eggs, then stir in the flour to make a fairly soft dough. Roll the dough into 40 small, evenly sized balls. Place on the prepared baking trays and flatten each ball slightly with the prongs of a fork. Press a peanut in the centre of each biscuit.

Bake the cookies in a moderate oven for 20-25 minutes or until golden brown. Using a palette knife, carefully remove the cookies from the trays and transfer them to a wire rack to cool completely.

### ◼ MICROWAVE TIP

*Microwave the fat, cocoa powder and syrup in a bowl 1-2 minutes on full power, stirring once. Add the remaining ingredients and continue as above.*

### ◼ FREEZER TIP

*For freshly made cookies form half the dough into a roll about 4 cm/1½ inches in diameter, wrap in foil and freeze. Defrost, cut into slices and cook as above.*

# FANCY CAKES

A special occasion calls for a cake to celebrate and you will find a suitable recipe in this chapter. There are cakes for Christmas, Valentine's day and Easter, as well as luscious gâteaux for adult birthdays and a very simple children's birthday cake. There are small cakes for party teas which taste superb but look almost too pretty to eat.

## 285 COFFEE AND HAZELNUT GATEAU

**Preparation time:**
25 minutes

**Cooking time:**
40 minutes

**Oven temperature:**
180 C, 350 F, gas 4

**Makes 1 cake**

**Total calories:**
5000

YOU WILL NEED:
*3 eggs*
*175 g/6 oz caster sugar*
*175 g/6 oz plain flour*
*1 tablespoon coffee essence*
*3 tablespoons brandy*
*450 ml/¾ pint double or whipping cream*
*100 g/4 oz hazelnuts, chopped*
FOR THE GLACÉ ICING
*225 g/8 oz icing sugar*
*1 tablespoon coffee essence*
*1 tablespoon water*

Line and grease a deep 18 cm/7 inch cake tin. Whisk the eggs and sugar until pale and thick. Fold in the flour and coffee essence.

Pour into the tin. Bake in a moderate oven for abut 40 minutes. Cool on a wire rack, then cut into three equal layers horizontally. Soak each layer with 1 tablespoon of brandy. Whip the cream until thick. Use a little to sandwich the cake together and coat the sides. Press the hazelnuts on the sides of the cake. For the glacé icing, mix together the icing sugar, coffee essence and water and pour on the top – be careful not to let it go down the sides of the cake. Pipe a border with the remaining cream.

## 286 CHRISTMAS CAKE

**Preparation time:**
30 minutes

**Cooking time:**
3½ hours

**Oven temperature:**
140 C, 275 F, gas 1

**Makes 1 cake**

**Total calories:**
7120

YOU WILL NEED:
*225 g/8 oz butter*
*225 g/8 oz light soft brown sugar*
*1 tablespoon black treacle*
*5 eggs*
*250 g/9 oz plain flour*
*1 teaspoon ground mixed spice*
*1 teaspoon grated nutmeg*
*50 g/2 oz ground almonds*
*grated rind of 1 lemon*
*grated rind of 1 orange*
*100 g/4 oz almonds, chopped*
*75 g/3 oz glacé cherries, chopped*
*175 g/6 oz raisins*
*250 g/9 oz sultanas*
*350 g/12 oz currants*
*100 g/4 oz chopped mixed peel*
*2 tablespoons brandy*
*2 tablespoons orange juice*

Line and grease a 23 cm/9 inch round cake tin or a 20 cm/8 inch square cake tin. Cream the butter and sugar until light and fluffy. Beat in the treacle, then the eggs, adding a little of the flour after the first one. Mix the remaining flour with all the dry ingredients. Fold into the creamed mixture. Stir in the brandy and orange juice. Turn into the tin and level the top. Protect the outside of the tin with newspaper. Bake in a cool oven for 3½ hours or until a metal skewer inserted into the cake comes out clean. Cool in the tin for 20 minutes, then turn out on to a wire rack to cool completely. Store wrapped in foil.

■ COOK'S TIP

*To test whether cake is cooked, press centre gently with fingers. If cooked, cake will spring back.*

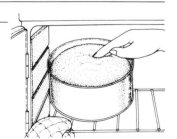

■ COOK'S TIP

*To keep cake for 3-4 months and to make it deliciously moist, prick top and bottom of cake with a skewer and spoon 2 tablespoons brandy over it every 2-3 weeks.*

# 287 ROYAL ICING

| Preparation time: | YOU WILL NEED: |
|---|---|
| 1 hour | FOR THE ALMOND PASTE |
| | 450 g/1 lb ground almonds |
| Covers 1 cake | 225 g/8 oz icing sugar |
| | 225 g/8 oz caster sugar |
| Total calories: | 2 teaspoons lemon juice |
| 8650 | 1 teaspoon almond essence |
| | 2 eggs, beaten |
| | 4 tablespoons apricot jam, sieved |
| | FOR THE ROYAL ICING |
| | 4 egg whites |
| | 1 kg/2 lb icing sugar, sifted twice |
| | 2 tablespoons glycerine |
| | a few drops of rose water |

For the almond paste, mix the dry ingredients. Add the lemon juice, almond essence and enough egg to make a stiff pliable dough. Knead briefly until smooth.

Brush the top of the cake with apricot jam. Roll out a third of the paste large enough to cover the cake top. Lift it on top of the cake, trim the edges. Smooth the top and edges evenly with fingertips. Roll the remaining paste into a strip the width of the side of the cake and long enough to go round the cake. Brush the sides of the cake with jam, then place the almond paste round the cake, smoothing on to the sides. Smooth all edges and joins. Leave for 1-2 weeks.

Lightly whisk the egg whites, then gradually beat in the icing sugar. Beat in the glycerine and rose water to make a smooth thick icing. Spread thickly over the sides of the cake and fork into peaks.

---

## ■ COOK'S TIP

To ice as shown, spread sides with three-quarters of icing, forking it up over top edge. Dry overnight. Keep remaining icing in an airtight container. Thin it by adding water, drop by drop, so that it will only just pour. Spoon icing on top, teasing it up to peaked edges with point of a knife to make a smooth top. Decorate when dry.

# 288 CHOCOLATE LOG

| Preparation time: | YOU WILL NEED: |
|---|---|
| 20 minutes | 3 eggs |
| | 75 g/3 oz caster sugar |
| Cooking time: | 2 tablespoons cocoa powder, sifted |
| 7-10 minutes | 65 g/2½ oz plain flour, sifted |
| Oven temperature: | FOR THE FILLING AND ICING |
| 220 C, 425 F, gas 7 | 100 g/4 oz butter or margarine |
| | 225 g/8 oz icing sugar |
| Makes 1 | 50 g/2 oz plain chocolate |
| Total calories: | holly leaves and icing sugar, to |
| 2711 | decorate |

Line and grease a 23 × 30 cm/9 × 12 inch Swiss roll tin. Whisk the eggs and sugar until pale and very thick (see recipe 271). Fold in the cocoa and flour with a metal spoon, then pour the mixture into the tin. Bake in a hot oven for 7-10 minutes.

Place a clean tea-towel on a work surface, cover with greaseproof paper and sprinkle with caster sugar. Turn the Swiss roll out on to the paper. Trim off the crusty edges and lay a sheet of greaseproof paper on top. Roll up tightly to enclose the paper. Cool.

Beat the butter or margarine and icing sugar until pale. Melt the chocolate in a basin over a saucepan of hot water and add it to the mixture. Unroll the cake, remove paper and spread with some buttercream. Roll up and cover with the remaining buttercream. Decorate as shown.

---

## ■ FREEZER TIP

Open freeze the cake until firm, then place in a polythene box. Remove from box and defrost at room temperature.

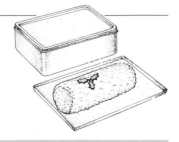

## 289 VALENTINE CAKE

**Preparation time:**
30 minutes

**Cooking time:**
35-40 minutes

**Oven temperature:**
180 C, 350 F, gas 4

**Makes 1 cake**

**Total calories:**
6170

YOU WILL NEED:
*175 g/6 oz butter or margarine*
*175 g/6 oz caster sugar*
*3 eggs*
*175 g/6 oz self-raising flour*
FOR THE FILLING AND ICING
*600 ml/1 pint double or whipping*
  *cream*
*4 tablespoons redcurrant jelly*
*100 g/4 oz icing sugar*
*1 tablespoon water*
*a few drops of pink food colouring*

Grease a 20 cm/8 inch heart-shaped cake tin. Cream the butter or margarine and sugar until light and fluffy. Gradually beat in the eggs, then fold in the flour.

Bake in a moderate oven for 35-40 minutes or until golden and firm. Turn out to cool on a wire rack. Cut the cake horizontally in half.

Whip the cream until thick. Sandwich the cake halves together with half the reducrrant jelly and some of the cream. Dissolve the remaining redcurrant jelly in a saucepan over a low heat, then smooth over the top of the cake. Cool. Pipe cream around the sides of the cake.

Beat the icing sugar with the water and food colouring until smooth. Pour over the jelly on top of the cake. Add a border of cream on the top of the cake.

## 290 EASTER CAKE

**Preparation time:**
30 minutes

**Cooking time:**
2 hours 50 minutes

**Oven temperature:**
160 C, 325 F, gas 3
and
150 C, 300 F, gas 2

**Makes 1 cake**

**Total calories:**
8215

YOU WILL NEED:
*175 g/6 oz butter or margarine*
*175 g/6 oz soft brown sugar*
*3 large eggs*
*225 g/8 oz self-raising flour*
*2 teaspoons mixed spice*
*350 g/12 oz sultanas*
*225 g/8 oz raisins*
*100 g/4 oz chopped mixed peel*
*50 g/2 oz blanched almonds, chopped*
*4-5 tablespoons milk*
*¾ quantity almond paste (recipe 287)*
*2 tablespoons apricot jam, sieved*
*1 egg white*

Line and grease a deep 20 cm/8 inch cake tin. Cream the butter or margarine and sugar until pale and soft. Gradually beat in the eggs adding a little of the flour. Fold in the remaining flour, spice, fruit, peel and nuts. Stir in milk to make a soft consistency. Spread half the mixture in the tin.

Roll a third of the almond paste into a 20 cm/8 inch circle. Place on top of the mixture, top with the remaining mixture; hollow out the centre slightly. Bake in a moderate oven for 1 hour, reduce to a cool oven for a further 1 hour 15 minutes (approx).

Cool in the tin for 15 minutes, then turn out on to a wire rack. Remove the paper. Brush the top of the cake with apricot jam. Roll half the remaining almond paste to fit the top of the cake. Roll the remainder into balls. Press the paste on the cake, adding the balls as shown. Brush with egg white and brown under the grill.

---

■ COOK'S TIP

*Cook this cake in a 20 cm/8 inch round cake tin and continue as above for a celebration cake for any occasion.*

■ FREEZER TIP

*To make jam easier to brush on cake, heat in a small bowl in the microwave with 1 teaspoon water for a few seconds, then sieve.*

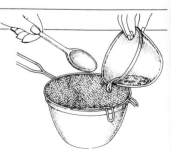

# 291 MOCHA GATEAU

**Preparation time:**
30 minutes

**Cooking time:**
25-30 minutes

**Oven temperature:**
190 C, 375 F, gas 5

**Makes 1 cake**

**Total calories:**
3875

YOU WILL NEED:
100 g/4 oz caster sugar
3 eggs
100 g/4 oz plain flour, sifted
25 g/1 oz cocoa powder, sifted
2 tablespoons brandy
FOR THE FILLING AND TOPPING
450 ml/¾ pint double cream
2 tablespoons sweetened strong black
    coffee
1 teaspoon cocoa powder
1 teaspoon instant coffee
2-3 teaspoons hot water
175 g/6 oz icing sugar, sifted
grated chocolate, to decorate

Grease a loose-bottomed 20 cm/8 inch deep round cake tin. Whisk the sugar and eggs together until pale and thick. Carefully fold in the sifted flour and cocoa powder. Pour into the cake tin and bake in a moderately hot oven for 15-20 minutes. Turn out on to a wire rack. When cool, split in half horizontally and sprinkle over the brandy.

Whip the cream and black coffee until stiff. Place a star nozzle in a piping bag and fill the bag with the coffee cream. Pipe swirls over one half of the cake, place on a serving plate and top with the other half. Pipe the remainder of the cream around the top of the gâteau.

Dissolve the cocoa and coffee in the water, then mix with the icing sugar to make glacé icing. Spread on top of the cake up to the cream border. Decorate with grated chocolate.

# 292 BIRTHDAY CAKE

**Preparation time:**
20 minutes

**Cooking time:**
1 hour 20 minutes

**Oven temperature:**
180 C, 350 F, gas 4

**Makes 1 cake**

**Total calories:**
6365

YOU WILL NEED:
175 g/6 oz butter or margarine
175 g/6 oz caster sugar
3 eggs, lightly beaten
225 g/8 oz self-raising flour
225 g/8 oz chocolate chips
a little milk, if necessary
FOR THE TOPPING
75 g/3 oz butter or margarine
225 g/8 oz icing sugar, sifted
1-2 tablespoons milk
a few drops of green food colouring
1 × 150 g/5¼ oz packet chocolate
    animals
FOR THE DECORATION
crêpe paper, spotty bow and candles

Line and grease a deep 18 cm/7 inch cake tin. Cream the butter or margarine and sugar until pale and fluffy. Gradually add the eggs. Fold in the flour and chocolate chips, adding a little milk to make a fairly stiff dropping consistency. Spoon into the tin and bake in a moderate oven for 1 hour 20 minutes. A metal skewer inserted into the cake should come out clean. Leave to cool in the tin for 5 minutes, then turn out to cool completely on a wire rack.

Beat the butter or margarine, sugar, milk and food colouring together. Spread over the top and sides of the cake and fork up. Decorate as shown. Finally, add the candles.

---

■ FREEZER TIP

This gâteau can be frozen without the glacé icing. Open freeze until firm, then wrap in a large polythene bag. Unwrap and defrost on a serving plate.

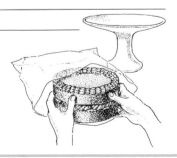

■ COOK'S TIP

To make a very quick, one-stage cake, use soft margarine and add 1 tablespoon baking powder to the ingredients. Beat all together until very soft and light. Stir in the chocolate chips last.

If the chocolate chips are not available, chop a bar of dark plain chocolate.

## 293 BATTENBURG CAKE

| | |
|---|---|
| **Preparation time:** 25 minutes | **YOU WILL NEED:** 175 g/6 oz butter or margarine |
| **Cooking time:** 35-40 minutes | 175 g/6 oz caster sugar<br>3 eggs<br>175 g/6 oz self-raising flour |
| **Oven temperature:** 180 C, 350 F, gas 4 | grated rind of 1 lemon<br>a few drops of pink food colouring |
| **Makes 1 cake** | 2 tablespoons lemon curd<br>450 g/1 lb marzipan |
| **Total calories:** 4990 | caster sugar, for dredging |

Line and grease a deep 18 cm/7 inch square cake tin and divide down the middle with a strip of folded greaseproof paper. Cream the fat and sugar until pale and fluffy. Gradually beat in the eggs, then fold in the flour.

Halve the mixture. Add the lemon rind to one portion and colouring to the other. Put mixtures separately in the tin. Bake in a moderate oven for 35-40 minutes or until a skewer inserted into the cake comes out clean. Cool on a wire rack.

Trim the edges, cut each piece of cake in half lengthways, making four strips. Sandwich alternate colours together with lemon curd in two layers. Roll the marzipan to a 20 × 37 cm/8 × 15 inch oblong. Spread the outide of the cake with lemon curd. Place in the middle of the marzipan. Ease the marzipan around the cake. With join underneath, pinch the edges and dust with caster sugar.

## 294 DEVIL'S FOOD CAKE

| | |
|---|---|
| **Preparation time:** 20 minutes | **YOU WILL NEED:** 175 g/6 oz butter or margarine |
| **Cooking time:** 2 hours | 175 g/6 oz caster sugar<br>3 eggs<br>4 tablespoons golden syrup |
| **Oven temperature:** 150 C, 300 F, gas 2 | 50 g/2 oz ground almonds<br>50 g/2 oz cocoa powder |
| **Makes 1 cake** | 175 g/6 oz self-raising flour<br>150 ml/¼ pint milk |
| **Total calories:** 4505 | grated chocolate, to decorate<br>*FOR THE FROSTING*<br>1 egg white<br>175 g/6 oz icing sugar<br>1 tablespoon golden syrup<br>3 tablespoons water |

Line and grease a deep 20 cm/8 inch round cake tin. Cream the butter or margarine and sugar until light and fluffy. Gradually beat in the eggs, then thoroughly stir in the syrup, almonds and cocoa powder. Carefully fold in the flour and add enough milk to make a mixture with a dropping consistency. Spoon into the tin, smooth the top and bake in a cool oven for about 2 hours. Turn out on to a wire rack to cool.

Make the frosting: place all the ingredients in a basin over boiling water and whisk until the icing stands in soft peaks. Remove from the heat and continue whisking until cool, then quickly spread it over the cake as shown. Decorate with grated chocolate.

■ MICROWAVE TIP

*To make lemon curd: cook the juice of 3 lemons with 100 g/4 oz butter and 350 g/ 12 oz caster sugar on full power for 6 minutes. Meanwhile, whisk 3 eggs and the grated rind of 3 lemons. Whisk in the hot butter. Cook for about 12-14 minutes, whisking every 2 minutes. Strain and pot.*

■ COOK'S TIP

*To line cake tin: cut circles of greaseproof paper the size of tin base. Cut a double thickness strip of paper 5 cm/ 2 in wider than height of tin and the length of the side.*

*Fold up 1 cm/½ in along length. Snip at intervals. Grease tin. Place strip around edge with folded edge on bottom of tin. Place two circles in tin. Grease.*

# 295 MARBLED CAKE

**Preparation time:**
25 minutes

**Cooking time:**
1 hour

**Oven temperature:**
160 C, 325 F, gas 3

**Makes 1 cake**

**Total calories:**
4635

YOU WILL NEED:
*175 g/6 oz butter or margarine*
*175 g/6 oz caster sugar*
*3 eggs*
*175 g/6 oz self-raising flour*
*green food colouring*
*pink food colouring*
FOR THE FILLING AND ICING
*50 g/2 oz cocoa powder*
*3 tablespoons boiling water*
*275 g/10 oz icing sugar*
*75 g/3 oz butter*
*chopped pistachio nuts, to decorate*

Line and grease a deep 18 cm/7 inch round cake tin. Cream the butter or margarine and sugar until pale and fluffy. Gradually beat in the eggs, then fold in the flour. Divide the mixture into three equal portions. Leave one portion plain, colour one green and the other pink. Drop spoonsful of the mixture in the tin, and carefully smooth the top without mixing the colours.

Bake in a moderate oven for about 1 hour or until a metal skewer inserted into the cake comes out clean. Cool on a wire rack. Dissolve the cocoa in the water; cool. Beat all the icing ingredients together and smooth half over the top and sides of the cake. Pipe a border with the remainder. Decorate with pistachio nuts.

# 296 SACHERTORTE

**Preparation time:**
20 minutes

**Cooking time:**
1 hour

**Oven temperature:**
180 C, 350 F, gas 4

**Makes 1 cake**

**Total calories:**
3610

YOU WILL NEED:
*100 g/4 oz plain chocolate*
*100 g/4 oz butter*
*4 eggs*
*100 g/4 oz icing sugar, sifted*
*50 g/2 oz self-raising flour*
*50 g/2 oz ground almonds*
FOR THE TOPPING
*225 g/8 oz plain chocolate*

Line and grease a deep 23 cm/9 inch round cake tin. Heat the chocolate and butter together in a bowl above a saucepan of hot, not boiling, water until melted. Cool slightly. Stir well and remove from the heat. Whisk together the eggs and icing sugar until pale and very thick. Fold in the chocolate and butter mixture, then fold in the flour and almonds. Pour the mixture into the prepared tin and bake in a moderate oven for about 1 hour, or until a metal skewer inserted into the centre of the cake comes out clean. Turn out on to a wire rack to cool. For the topping, melt the chocolate, and quickly smooth over the cake with a palette knife. Leave to cool. Decorate as shown.

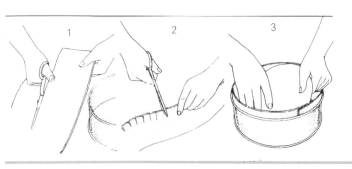

**MICROWAVE TIP**

*To melt chocolate in the microwve, break into squares and place in a bowl. Microwave for 4-6 minutes until soft.*

## 297 TREACLE CAKE

**Preparation time:**
20 minutes

**Cooking time:**
1 hour

**Oven temperature:**
180 C, 350 F, gas 4

**Makes 1 cake**

**Total calories:**
4955

YOU WILL NEED:
175 g/6 oz butter or margarine
175 g/6 oz caster sugar
3 tablespoons black treacle
3 eggs
350 g/12 oz self-raising flour
2 tablespoons milk
FOR THE ICING
50 g/2 oz butter or margarine
1 tablespoon black treacle
1 tablespoon milk
225 g/8 oz icing sugar, sifted

Line and grease a deep 20 cm/8 inch square cake tin. Cream the butter or margarine, sugar and treacle together until light and fluffy. Gradually beat in the eggs, adding a tablespoon of flour if necessary to prevent the mixture from curdling. Carefully fold in the flour and milk. Spoon the mixture into the prepared tin and bake in a moderate oven for 1 hour or until a metal skewer inserted into the cake comes out clean. Cool on a wire rack. Beat all icing ingredients together until smooth. Swirl on cake as shown.

## 298 CHOCOLATE REFRIGERATOR CAKE

**Preparation time:**
10 minutes, plus 1 hour to chill

**Cooking time:**
5 minutes

**Makes 1 cake**

**Total calories:**
4660

YOU WILL NEED:
450 g/1 lb plain chocolate
100 g/4 oz butter or margarine
2 tablespoons brandy
225 g/8 oz chocolate digestive biscuits, crushed
100 g/4 oz hazelnuts, chopped

Line and grease a deep 18 cm/7 inch square cake tin. Break the chocolate into small pieces and place in a basin with the butter over a saucepan of hot water. Heat gently until the chocolate and butter are melted. Remove from the heat, then stir in the brandy, biscuits and hazelnuts. Mix thoroughly, pour into the prepared tin and leave to cool. When cool, mark into twelve equal squares and refrigerate for 1 hour or until set. Cut into squares to serve.

### ■ COOK'S TIP

*When a cake is cooked in a tin lined with paper, remove paper when cake is turned out to cool unless storing cake for several days, when it can be left on.*

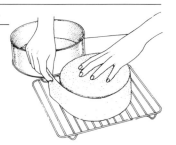

### ■ COOK'S TIP

*To crush biscuits, place in a paper bag and roll gently with a rolling pin.*

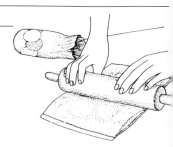

# 299 TIPSY RING

**Preparation time:**
15 minutes

**Cooking time:**
40-50 minutes

**Oven temperature:**
160 C, 325 F, gas 3

**Makes 1 cake**

**Total calories:**
2600

YOU WILL NEED:
*100 g/4 oz butter or margarine*
*100 g/4 oz caster sugar*
*2 eggs*
*100 g/4 oz self-raising flour*
*25 g/1 oz cocoa powder*
*1 tablespoon instant coffee dissolved*
*    in 1 tablespoon boiling water*
*2 tablespoons brandy*
*FOR THE GLACÉ ICING*
*175 g/6 oz icing sugar, sifted*
*25 g/1 oz cocoa powder*
*1 tablespoon instant coffee dissolved*
*    in 1 tablespoon boiling water*
*1 tablespoon brandy*

Grease a 23 cm/9 inch ring tin. Cream together the butter or margarine and sugar until light and fluffy. Gradually beat in the eggs, then carefully fold in the flour, cocoa powder and coffee mixture. Spoon the mixture into the prepared tin and bake in a moderate oven for 40-50 minutes or until a metal skewer inserted into the cake comes out clean.

While the cake is still hot, pour 2 tablespoons brandy evenly over it. Leave for 5 minutes, then turn out and cool on a wire rack. For the icing, beat all the ingredients together and drizzle over the top of the cake.

# 300 CHOCOLATE CUPS

**Preparation time:**
25 minutes, plus 1 hour to chill

**Cooking time:**
5 minutes

**Makes 8**

**Calories:**
505 per cake

YOU WILL NEED:
*225 g/8 oz plain chocolate*
*225 g/8 oz chocolate or coffee cake,*
*    crumbled*
*1 tablespoon cocoa powder*
*2 tablespoons rum or sherry*
*50 g/2 oz chopped mixed nuts*
*1 tablespoon chocolate spread*
*300 ml/½ pint double or whipping*
*    cream*
*chopped nuts, to decorate*

Place eight double thickness paper cases (one case inside another) on a wire rack. Heat the chocolate in a basin over a saucepan of hot, not boiling, water until melted. Brush the chocolate fairly thickly around the insides of the cases, then leave to cool and set.

Meanwhile, mix together the cake crumbs, cocoa powder, rum or sherry and nuts.

When the chocolate has set, carefully peel off the paper cases, and fill the chocolate cups with the mixture. Mix the chocolate spread with 2 tablespoons of the cream. Whip the remaining cream until thick, then fold in the chocolate mixture.

Spoon into a piping bag fitted with a star nozzle and pipe swirls of chocolate cream on the top of the cake mixture and decorate with chopped nuts. Chill before serving.

■ MICROWAVE TIP

*To soften refrigerator-hard fat for creaming for cakes or for spreading, heat in microwave for 1-2 minutes.*

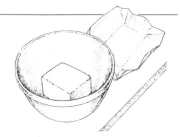

■ COOK'S TIP

*When melting chocolate be careful not to over-heat it or it will go grainy. Take care not to get any water in the chocolate, always dry bottom of bowl.*

## 301 ICED FANCIES

**Preparation time:**
25 minutes

**Cooking time:**
7-10 minutes

**Oven temperature:**
220 C, 425 F, gas 7

**Makes 16**

**Calories:**
210 per cake

YOU WILL NEED:
*3 eggs*
*75 g/3 oz caster sugar*
*75 g/3 oz plain flour*
*FOR THE GLACÉ ICING*
*225 g/8 oz icing sugar, sifted*
*2 tablespoons warm water*
*a few drops of food colouring*
*FOR THE BUTTERCREAM*
*100 g/4 oz butter*
*225 g/8 oz icing sugar*
*1-2 tablespoons milk*
*1 drop vanilla essence*
*a few drops of food colouring*
*FOR THE DECORATION*
*silver balls, crystallized fruit, grated*
  *chocolate or nuts*

Line and grease a 30 × 18 × 3 cm/12 × 7 × 1¼ inch tin. Whisk the eggs and sugar until pale and very thick. Carefully fold in the flour, using a metal spoon. Pour the mixture into the tin and bake in a hot oven for 7-10 minutes. Turn out on a sheet of greaseproof paper on a wire rack to cool.

Use a variety of cutters to cut out shapes from the sponge. For the glacé icing, beat all the ingredients thoroughly. The icing can be coloured if liked. Ice the cakes.

Beat the butter, sugar, milk and vanilla together until smooth. Colour if liked, and pipe on the cakes. Decorate as shown.

## 302 MERINGUE SNOWMEN

**Preparation time:**
30 minutes

**Cooking time:**
2 hours

**Oven temperature:**
110 C, 225 F, gas ¼

**Makes 20**

**Calories:**
90 per snowman

YOU WILL NEED:
*4 egg whites*
*225 g/8 oz caster sugar*
*FOR THE FILLING*
*150 ml/¼ pint double or whipping*
  *cream*
*FOR THE DECORATION*
*chocolate drops*
*red bootlace liquorice*
*sticks of liquorice*
*1 packet liquorice allsorts*
*rice paper*
*a few drops of food colouring*

Grease three baking trays. Whisk the egg whites until stiff but not dry, then gradually whisk in the sugar to make a stiff glossy mixture. Using two wet tablespoons, put spoonsful of the mixture on the trays. Using wet teaspoons, put the same number of spoonsful of the mixture on the trays. Bake in a very cool oven for 2 hours, until dry. Cool on a wire rack.

Whip the cream until thick. Sandwich the large shapes together with cream to make the bodies and the small shapes to make the heads. Use cream to stick the snowmen together. Using a piping bag and a star nozzle, pipe on the features. Decorate as shown. Make hats from circles of rice paper. Cut a hole in the centre and place a liquorice allsort in the middle.

■ FREEZER TIP

*Place cut-out shapes on a wire rack and freeze, to prevent cakes crumbling when glacé icing is spooned over.*

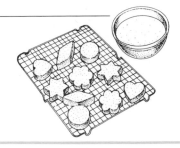

■ FREEZER TIP

*Egg yolks freeze well. Beat with either a pinch of salt or ½ teaspoon sugar and store in small pots. Mark on pots how many yolks and whether sweet or savoury.*

## 303 RASPBERRY CREAM SQUARES

**Preparation time:**
25 minutes

**Cooking time:**
10-12 minutes

**Oven temperature:**
220 C, 425 F, gas 7

**Calories:**
575 per square

YOU WILL NEED:
1 × 368 g/13 oz packet puff pastry
2 tablespoons raspberry jam, sieved
300 ml/½ pint double or whipping cream
50 g/2 oz raspberries
100 g/4 oz icing sugar
1 tablespoon water

Grease two baking trays. Roll out the pastry thinly and cut into two 7.5 × 30 cm/3 × 12 inch strips. Place on the prepared baking trays and bake in a hot oven for 10-12 minutes or until well risen and golden. Leave to cool on a wire rack. Heat the jam until runny and brush on to one strip of pastry. Whip the cream until thick, then fold in the raspberries. Spread the cream filling over the pastry slice without the jam. Top with the jam-coated pastry slice, jam side up. Carefully cut into four. Beat the icing sugar and water until smooth and pour over the jam.

## 304 GINGER SNAPS

**Preparation time:**
25 minutes

**Cooking time:**
8-10 minutes

**Oven temperature:**
190 C, 375 F, gas 5

**Makes 12**

**Calories:**
130 per ginger snap

YOU WILL NEED:
50 g/2 oz butter or margarine
2 tablespoons syrup
50 g/2 oz soft brown sugar
50 g/2 oz plain flour
1 teaspoon ground ginger
FOR THE FILLING
150 ml/¼ pint double or whipping cream
chopped stem ginger and angelica, to decorate

Grease as many wooden spoon handles as possible. Thoroughly grease two baking trays. Melt the butter or margarine, syrup and sugar over a low heat, then stir in the flour and ginger. Drop teaspoonsful of the mixture well apart on a baking tray to allow room for spreading.

Cook in a moderately hot oven for 8-10 minutes, then leave the biscuits to cool for a few seconds. Use a palette knife to lift them off very carefully, then roll around the wooden spoon handles with the top of the biscuit on the outside. Hold in position for a few minutes until set. Slip the biscuits from the handles and place on a wire rack to cool. Bake the biscuits in batches. If they set too quickly return them to the oven for a few seconds to melt.

Whip the cream until thick and use to fill the ginger snaps. Decorate with stem ginger and angelica.

### ■ COOK'S TIP

For custard slices: spread both slices of cooked pastry with jam and thick custard with whipped cream folded in. Sandwich together, jam sides in. Cut into slices.

### ■ COOK'S TIP

To make cups to hold ice cream or sorbet, mould hot biscuits over oiled oranges and leave to cool.

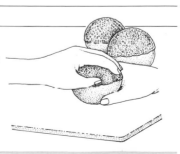

# INDEX